WEEKLY
PROVISIONS

DK | Penguin Random House

Publishing Director Katie Cowan
Art Director Maxine Pedliham
Senior Acquisitions Editor Stephanie Milner
Managing Art Editor Bess Daly
Project Editor Judy Barratt
Project Designer Georgina Hewitt
Proofreader Anne Sheasby
Indexer Hilary Bird
Jackets Coordinator Lucy Philpott
Photographer Yuki Sugiura
Food Stylist Valerie Berry
Prop Stylist Alexander Breeze
Illustrator Anisa Makhoul
Production Editor Heather Blagden
Production Controller Rebecca Parton

First published in Great Britain in 2021 by
Dorling Kindersley Limited
DK, One Embassy Gardens, 8 Viaduct Gardens,
London, SW11 7BW

The authorised representative in the EEA is
Dorling Kindersley Verlag GmbH.
Arnulfstr. 124, 80636 Munich, Germany

A CIP catalogue record for this book
is available from the British Library.
ISBN: 978-0-2415-0315-7

Printed and bound in Latvia

For the curious
www.dk.com

Cook's Notes

Unless otherwise specified:
Use fresh, medium-sized fruit and vegetables
Use medium eggs
Use a flavourless oil, such as sunflower, rapeseed
  or vegetable
Use level tablespoons and teaspoons

Serves are average portion sizes per person;
timings are approximations to active cooking
+ making time in the method, after ingredient
preparation.

To deep-fry, choose a heavy-based saucepan of a
size in which the oil comes two thirds of the way
up the sides. Do not overfill. Protect your hands
and take care of scalding oil.

To store, allow ingredients to cool before sealing
and refrigerating or freezing. If cooking a remix
from frozen ingredients, you may need to
increase the suggested cooking time. Always test
for doneness before eating.

This book was made with Forest Stewardship Council ™ certified
paper – one small step in DK's commitment to a sustainable future.
For more information go to www.dk.com/our-green-pledge

WEEKLY
PROVISIONS

How to eat seasonally and love what's left over

Kim Duke

Contents

Weekly Provisions

For as long as I can remember, I've been obsessed with food. Some of my earliest memories are of making vanilla toffee with my dad and picking peas in my grandad's little greenhouse. I was always so intrigued with the processes, the smells and the colours. When I was very young, my dad would cut up potatoes to make stamps for my sister and me to paint with. I think it was perhaps through all those experiences that I learned that food can be many things: sustenance, but also playful and fun. In this book, I've tried to make that my motto. The pages are filled with recipes that are delicious and adventurous, but I hope they are always practical and plentiful; that they feed you today, but also tomorrow, or the day after.

When I was younger, we didn't have much money. Mum would send my sister and me to school in the mornings with 50p for breakfast and a little bag of cereal to snack on. I would start the day with a pink sprinkle donut from the local bakery; my sister would have a sausage roll. We never felt poor with such decadence every morning. But, what was always made clear to us was that wasting food wasn't an option: we always needed to make sure we ate up everything on our plates, or save it for later. Now, I love to save a little bit of this and that when I'm cooking, in the hope I can make something delicious with it another time.

Food can be many things – sustenance, but also playful and fun

And that's how this book was born. If you love to eat (and love to eat decadently), but also feel an intrinsic responsibility to love what you make and not to waste a crumb, then this book is for you.

The book is organized seasonally, in part as a nod to the spirit of reducing waste – many of the dishes include ingredients that are best harvested or eaten at a particular time of year. But, sometimes, for me a dish is less about what's in it and more about how it makes me feel – the memories and passions it conjures up and how they speak to me about a particular time of year. I've used both these approaches to choosing my menus, so you'll have to forgive me if occasionally you find yourself sourcing hazelnuts in spring, say, or strawberries in winter. We are so lucky to be able to get almost all ingredients at any time of the year, and that means I can indulge my deep need to make and eat food that brings me comfort not only because of the flavours, but also because of the significance each dish has for me. In a sense, then, this is a deeply personal book – and I'm so happy to share it with you.

Summer is where we begin, with menus that are fresh and zesty, and light but hearty, in homage to the warmer months. From there, we move through the seasons in order – autumn bringing root vegetables, spicy curries, and Chinese dumplings (which are as therapeutic to make as they are to eat). In winter, we turn inward with long roasts and hearty puddings that epitomize the days when all you want to do is keep warm indoors and envelop yourself in flavour (or, is that just me?). And last to spring – the season of renewed energy to round off the book, reflected in dishes that celebrate all that is good in a food-lover's life – for me, seafood, new-season lamb, and an overall passion for indulging in world cuisine. In each season there are plenty of vegetarian options for those who want to eat more sustainably; and there are vegan dishes, too. I defy any meat-eater not to love them all!

Within each seasonal chapter, three menus provide three bountiful feasts – these are dishes (starters, mains, sides and desserts) worth setting the table for. Most menus feed four people and are intended to share with friends and family, but I've also included menus for two – because sometimes one significant other (be it

For me, a dish is less about what's in it and more about how it makes me feel

a best friend, a family member or a lover) is all you need.

Each dish in the menus intentionally provides enough leftovers to make some other beautiful and delicious things far beyond the original supper. These are the remixes: at the end of each menu is a coloured section of recipes that take what you've already made for your feast and reinvent it into something else you can eat during the week. This way, nothing is wasted and good, tasty food and sweet morsels are easier to rustle up on days when you're too busy to think creatively, but know you want something home-cooked and then need something sweet.

Among the remixes you'll find a mixture of breakfasts, lunches, dinners and treats, as well as several syrups that you can repurpose for a delicious chai latte, or pour over ice cream, or turn into a banana caramel milkshake – among other things. One of my favourite menus, found in spring, is "Northern (Street)lights, the Taste of Home", which is dedicated to my home in the north of England. It provides the perfect example for how creative you can be from just one dish. The main in this menu is a gorgeous honey and bay roasted ham. It will serve four for dinner, but also give you leftovers to make a supper of Hawaiian fried rice during the week, ham stock potatoes, as a side, and a jambon beurre – the perfect deli sandwich for lunch.

I've tried as far as I can to make sure the recipes, especially the remixes, use additional ingredients you'll already have in your cupboards (pasta, rice, dried spices and seasonings), or that you can pick up easily in supermarkets to become storecupboard staples – as well as fresh fruit, veg and meat, of course. Occasionally, there are recipes that require something more unusual – if you have no luck in the supermarket, please don't give up because I promise every ingredient is worth tracking down. Try online, which has opened up a whole world of flavour that makes cooking and eating so much more exciting today than it has ever been.

I want you to enjoy this book your way

An important thing: although the menu recipes are arranged to work together and as a starter, main and dessert, and even though the book is organized by season – please don't think you can't mix and match, explore and experiment. Equally, even though the remixes call for ingredients in a recipe you've already made, in most cases you can easily swap in something that you buy on the day. In short, if you want to have chorizo and fennel jam on toast for a starter, with paneer and lentil curry for a main and peach melba tart for dessert, I wholeheartedly encourage you to do so! If the aim is to create a three-course dinner that will give you the most substantial leftovers for the week – go for it. I won't stop you; I want you to enjoy this book your way.

Equally, please don't get too bogged down with specific ingredients – be bold, change it up. If the recipe calls for kale, but you can only get chard, that's okay. Or, if you don't fancy lamb but you want to try the black garlic glaze, use chicken instead. Cooking and eating can be so much fun if we approach it with childlike curiosity. And if your tart doesn't turn out exactly like the picture, or your croquettes are a little oblong rather than round – all the better. (I can't count how many times I've made a leaky croquette and enjoyed it abundantly in the kitchen, on my own, waiting for the others to fry.) Cooking isn't about perfection. Cooking is something to undertake slowly and as an act of self-love. It's sustenance, yes, but it's so much more. Enjoy this book whenever and however you can. Think of it as just the start.

Cooking isn't about perfection. Cooking is something to undertake slowly and as an act of self-love

Kim

Summer

For me, summer eating is about fresh seafood, potato salads, sweet and spicy condiments; it's about sharing meals that are light, but don't compromise on flavour. In addition, when it's hot I don't want to spend hours in the kitchen, so having the opportunity for some quick and easy remixes to keep me properly fed with minimal effort during the week just about seems perfect.

The first menu in this chapter – which I've called **Subtle spice, sea and sun** – is a showcase for my favourite summer foods, starting with soft and delicately flavoured crab cakes with crispy curry leaves. As soon as the sun comes out, I crave juicy prawns, which in this menu are dusted with za'atar spice and served with a homemade sweet chilli sauce (just the right amount of heat). Aromatic, super-easy baked tomato and cinnamon rice, and longstem broccoli to make a substantial main course. The peach melba tart is a childhood favourite and makes a beautiful centrepiece for the dinner table. But if summer's juiciest, ripest peaches aren't your thing, feel free to swap in another soft fruit – strawberries or pitted cherries would also work particularly well.

I have to admit I've been a bit naughty with my second summer menu (**Fruits of the Earth**). I've included Jerusalem artichokes, which are more likely to become seasonal at the very end of summer and into autumn. But, bear with me – the decision to put them here is a personal one; and, in fact, the whole menu highlights the important links between food and happy memories for me. The first time I ate Jerusalem artichokes was in the late summer, on a rooftop in a pub where I used to work. I'd ordered them from our supplier because they intrigued me, but being a bit out of season, they were slightly more expensive than usual. It meant I had to do something special with them – bring on the confit artichokes with butter, garlic and onions. Truly amazing – and now you can make them, too (and none goes to waste because they're reimagined as artichoke risotto for the week). The Spinach and Feta Custard Pie reminds me of discovering beautiful bakeries in Greece; the "Everything Seasoning" Potatoes are inspired by the most deliciously spiced bagels I once bought during a sweltering summer in Soho, London (they were so good, I concluded that the flavour needed to be on everything); and the Tonka Bean Tres Leches Cake reminds me of blistering Mexico – the very place I first tried it. So, while not every ingredient might immediately scream summer to you, this menu is everything that says summer to me.

We're back to seafood for my final menu – **All rivers lead to the ocean** – with scallops for a starter and monkfish for a main (feel free to swap it for any other firm white fish, if you prefer). The herby crust on the monkfish – mint, parsley, dill – is the very essence of fresh flavour that cuts through summer heat, but it's the vegetables served up alongside that are the real stars of the show. Ginger and garlic, cooked at a high heat, give a wonderful smoky aroma to spring greens, which despite the name are still peaking during early summer. And for dessert? The coconut flavour of kaya jam and the zing of pineapple need no explanation – it's summer and so tropical flavours speak for themselves.

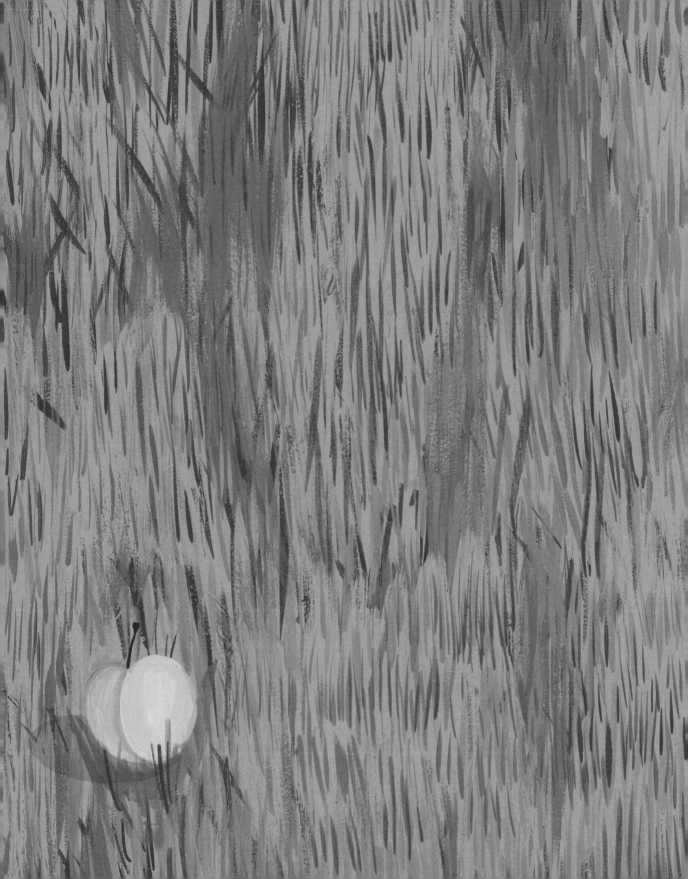

Summer

Menu one
Subtle spice, sea and sun

Menu two
Fruits of the Earth

Menu three
All rivers lead to the ocean

Remixes

Remixes

Remixes

Malted Crab Cakes *with* Crispy Curry Leaves

Makes 8–10

20 minutes

1 small courgette (zucchini), grated

100g (3½oz) cooked white crab meat

a small bunch of chives, chopped

1 teaspoon garlic powder

1 teaspoon onion powder

½ teaspoon ground white pepper

2 tablespoons malt vinegar

90g (3oz) self-raising flour

150g (5½oz) fresh breadcrumbs
   (or use panko)

90ml (3fl oz) flavourless oil

10 fresh curry leaves

For the curried mayonnaise

120g (4¼oz) mayonnaise

1 tablespoon roasted curry powder

½ teaspoon maple syrup

½ teaspoon malt vinegar

salt and freshly ground black pepper

01 First, make the mayonnaise. Place all the ingredients in a mixing bowl, season with salt and pepper and whisk until fully combined. Cover and refrigerate until you're ready to serve.

02 Make the crab cakes. Squeeze the excess water from the grated courgette (zucchini) and place the squeezed flesh into a mixing bowl. Add all the remaining ingredients except the breadcrumbs, oil and curry leaves, and mix well to fully incorporate the flour.

03 Place the breadcrumbs on a plate or baking tray. Get another plate ready to put the crab cakes on to once they are breaded.

04 Using a large tablespoon, scoop up a small ball of the crab mixture, a little bit smaller than a golf ball, and use another spoon to push it on to the breadcrumbs, flattening it slightly as you do so. Use one spoon to turn the crab in the breadcrumbs to coat, then pick up the crab cake and pop it on to the other plate ready for frying. Repeat until you have 8–10 balls.

05 Place a large frying pan over a high heat and add the oil. Line a plate with kitchen paper ready to receive the balls as they are cooked.

06 Once the oil is hot, add the curry leaves and fry for about 30 seconds – be careful as the oil may spit – to release their flavour. Remove the curry leaves from the pan and set aside. In two batches, add the crab cakes to the pan, gently pressing them down. Fry for about 1–2 minutes on each side, until nicely browned all over. Transfer the cooked crab cakes to the lined plate to drain for a few minutes. Transfer to a serving platter, scatter over the fried curry leaves and serve with the mayonnaise alongside.

Za'atar
Prawns

Serves 4

40 minutes

3 eggs

50ml (1¾fl oz) whole milk

3 tablespoons za'atar

1 teaspoon onion powder

1 teaspoon garlic powder

12 large fresh, peeled prawns (shrimp)

50g (1¾oz) potato or rice flour

250ml (9fl oz) flavourless oil, for deep frying

juice and finely grated zest of 1 lemon

salt and freshly ground black pepper

For the sweet chilli jam

5 roasted red (bell) peppers, from a jar

2 long red chillies

2 long green chillies

90g (3oz) caster (superfine) sugar

90ml (3fl oz) white vinegar

01 First, make the jam. Place all the ingredients into a food processor and blitz until roughly chopped.

02 Tip the mixture into a small saucepan with 2 teaspoons of water and place it over a high heat. Bring the mixture to a boil and allow to boil for 10 minutes, stirring occasionally, until the jam is glossy and thick. Turn off the heat. ***This will make enough jam also for the One-tray Chilli Chicken with Creamed Greens (see page 27). To store, transfer the jam to a sterilized jar, seal and cool. Refrigerate for up to 2 weeks.***

03 Make the prawns (shrimp). Break the eggs into a large mixing bowl. Add the milk, 1 tablespoon of the za'atar, and the onion and garlic powders and season with salt and pepper. Use a balloon whisk to fully combine. Tip in the prawns and stir to coat.

04 Tip the flour into a separate bowl and get a plate ready for the coated prawns.

05 One by one, pick up the prawns and shake off any excess egg mixture. Place each prawn into the flour and coat, making sure the flour sticks well. If you like, use a gloved hand to squeeze the coated prawn gently, which will give a crunchy flour coating. Set aside on the plate.

06 Once you have coated all the prawns, pour the oil into a heavy-based saucepan so that it comes two-thirds of the way up the sides. Heat it over a medium–low heat until it reaches 180°C (350°F) on a cooking thermometer. (Alternatively, use a deep-fat fryer.) To test the heat of the oil, drop in a little bit of flour. If it sizzles and browns quickly, the oil is ready.

07 Deep-fry the prawns in batches of 3 or 4 at a time for 2–3 minutes per batch, turning until golden and crispy all over. Using a slotted spoon, remove the cooked prawns and set aside to drain on kitchen paper.

08 Once all the prawns are cooked, sprinkle over the lemon juice and scatter over the remaining za'atar and the lemon zest. Season to taste.

Tomato
Baked Rice

Serves 4

50 minutes

20 cherry tomatoes

2 teaspoons garam masala or medium
     curry powder

1 teaspoon ground cinnamon

1 teaspoon ground turmeric

2 tablespoons garlic paste

90ml (3fl oz) flavourless oil

400g (14oz) jasmine or white basmati rice

01 Preheat the oven to 200°C (180°C fan/400°F/Gas 6).

02 Place the tomatoes in a baking dish and add the spices, garlic paste, and oil. Stir to combine. Bake for 10–12 minutes, until the tomatoes burst slightly.

03 Meanwhile, rinse the rice under cold running water until the water runs clear. When the tomatoes are ready, add the rice to the baking dish. Stir well, then add 200ml (7fl oz) of water. Stir again and cover with foil, or with a lid if you have one.

04 Bake the dish for 25–30 minutes, until the rice is slightly crispy on top and fluffy and tender underneath. ***To make the Smoked Haddock Kedgeree (see page 28), transfer one third of the rice to an airtight container. Refrigerate for up to 1 day.*** Serve the remainder straight from the dish.

Longstem Broccoli *with* Red Pepper Hummus

Serves 4

15 minutes

20 longstem broccoli, trimmed
salt

For the red pepper hummus

1 x 400g can of chickpeas (garbanzos),
    drained and rinsed
1 roasted red (bell) pepper, from a jar
1 teaspoon dried chilli flakes
1 garlic clove
1 teaspoon ground cumin (optional)
90ml (3fl oz) light tahini
90ml (3fl oz) extra-virgin olive oil
3 teaspoons sumac (optional)

01 Bring a large saucepan of salted water to a boil. Add the broccoli and cook for 2–3 minutes, until the stems are limp and tender. Drain in a colander, then transfer to a bowl and cover with cold water. Set aside while you make the hummus.

02 Tip the chickpeas (garbanzos), red (bell) pepper, chilli flakes, garlic clove and cumin (if using) into a food processor and blitz for 1–2 minutes until roughly chopped. Then, little by little, add the tahini, followed by the olive oil, blitzing between each addition until silky and smooth. *To make the Ultimate Broccoli Sub (see page 30), spoon 6 tablespoons of the hummus into an airtight container. Refrigerate for up to 2 days.*

03 Drain the broccoli and pat it roughly dry with kitchen paper. *To make the Ultimate Broccoli Sub, transfer 8 broccoli stems to an airtight container. Refrigerate for up to 2 days.* Spread the remaining hummus in a layer over a serving platter. Top with the remaining 12 stems of broccoli. Sprinkle over the sumac (if using) and serve.

Peach
Melba Tart

Serves 8

50 minutes

For the filling

6 peaches, stoned and diced

4 tablespoons caster (superfine) sugar

30 raspberries

300ml (10fl oz) double (heavy) cream

4 drops of almond extract

To assemble

80g (3oz) ready-to-roll white fondant icing

4 drops of natural orange food colouring
    (optional)

1 x 215g shop-bought sweet-pastry tart case

01 Place the diced peaches into a medium saucepan with 3 tablespoons of water and 1 tablespoon of the sugar. Cook over a medium heat, for about 10 minutes, until most of the water has evaporated and the peaches are shiny and soft. Tip the peaches and remaining liquid into a heatproof bowl and set aside for later.

02 Tip 18–20 of the raspberries and 2 tablespoons of the remaining sugar into the saucepan, along with 120ml (4fl oz) of water, and place over a medium heat. Stir well, then cook for about 10 minutes, until the liquid has reduced, the raspberries have broken down and you have a thick sauce. Remove from the heat and leave to cool.

03 Prepare the fondant icing. Lay out a sheet of greaseproof paper on your work surface. Lightly press out the fondant with your fingertips. Add the food colouring (if using) and knead the colour into the fondant until it is an even, peachy orange. Using a rolling pin, roll out the fondant to a 25cm (10in) disc, about 3mm (1/8in) thick. Place the pastry case on top of the fondant and cut around it to size. Set aside.

04 Pour the cream into a large bowl. Add the remaining 1 tablespoon of sugar and the almond extract and, using an electric hand whisk, whisk to stiff peaks. Spoon the cream into a disposable piping (pastry) bag, twist the top to seal and refrigerate for 10 minutes for the cream to firm up.

05 To assemble the tart, place the tart base on a serving plate and spoon in a layer of the peaches. Add a thin layer of the raspberry sauce on top. ***To make the Peach Melba Sundae (see page 31), transfer any leftover peaches and remaining raspberry sauce each into its own airtight container. Refrigerate for up to 4 days.***

06 Snip the end off the piping bag to make a 1cm (1/2in) hole. Pipe small mounds of cream in concentric circles to cover the filling.

07 Using a rolling pin to help you, carefully lift the fondant icing and lay it over the cream layer. Gently smooth the icing over the mounds of cream and place the remaining raspberries into the dips to decorate.

CURRY LEAF POPCORN

Curry leaves are one of those fresh ingredients that you tend to buy for a specific recipe, like the Malted Crab Cakes with Crispy Curry Leaves on page 18, but then never need the whole bunch. This simple recipe is the perfect snack for movie night – and a fabulous way to use up the remainder.

Serves 3–4   15 minutes

1 tablespoon flavourless oil
6–10 fresh curry leaves
1 teaspoon roasted garam masala
2 teaspoons caster (superfine) sugar
100g (3½oz) dried corn kernels
½ teaspoon ground cinnamon

01 Drizzle the oil into a large frying pan over a medium heat. Leave to heat up for 1 minute, then add the curry leaves. Fry for 15–20 seconds, until they crisp up, then remove them from the pan and set aside to drain on kitchen paper.

02 Place the drained curry leaves, garam masala and sugar in a large serving bowl and gently combine with a spoon – you can break up the curry leaves if you like, or leave them whole.

03 Tip the corn kernels into the pan you used to cook the leaves over a low heat. Place a lid on the pan (or cover with a piece of foil) and allow the kernels to cook for 4–6 minutes, until they start to pop. You can shake the pan gently to make sure that all of the kernels are cooked, if you like.

04 Once the pops become more spaced out (every 3 seconds or so), turn off the heat and remove the lid. Tip the hot popcorn into the serving bowl with the curry-leaf mixture, add the cinnamon and toss to coat.

ONE-TRAY CHILLI CHICKEN WITH CREAMED GREENS

I love that feeling, at the end of a long day, when I remember I've left myself the gorgeous gift of homemade sweet chilli jam already tucked away in the fridge. Just grab some chicken thighs, greens – I like cavolo nero for this – and a few extra fridge staples and you have the most delicious midweek dinner. If you don't have any garlic, use garlic powder (which you needed for the Za'atar Prawns); and if you don't have any cream, the greens are just as delicious without.

Serves 2   50 minutes

8 stems of cavolo nero, stalks discarded,
    leaves sliced into 1cm (½in) strips
1 red (bell) pepper, deseeded and sliced
    into 1cm (½in) strips
4 bone-in, skin-on chicken thighs
6 tablespoons sweet chilli jam from
    Za'atar Prawns (see page 20)
2 tablespoons flavourless oil
2 garlic cloves, finely chopped
4 tablespoons double (heavy) cream
salt and freshly ground black pepper

01 Preheat the oven to 220°C (200°C fan/ 425°F/Gas 7).

02 Place the strips of cavolo nero and red (bell) pepper in a baking tray.

03 Place the chicken thighs on top and spoon over the sweet chilli jam to coat the chicken. Sprinkle over the oil and season with salt.

04 Bake the chicken for 30 minutes, then remove from the oven and scatter over the garlic. Return to the oven for 10 minutes, until the chicken is cooked through.

05 Remove from the oven and transfer the chicken thighs to a plate. Keep warm.

06 Add the cream to the tray with the greens and peppers and stir well to combine. Divide the mixture between two serving plates and place 2 chicken thighs on top of each serving. Season with salt and pepper, then serve.

Summer

SMOKED HADDOCK KEDGEREE

Kedgeree is traditionally eaten as a breakfast dish, but I think if ever there were a perfect candidate for breakfast for dinner, this would be it. If you don't have any leftover baked rice from the previous days – because, let's face it, it was really good – you could instead use a pouch of the pre-cooked rice you can get in supermarkets. Try a Mediterranean-flavoured version to make sure you still get that little bit of extra something.

Serves 2   15–20 minutes

1 tablespoon flavourless oil
100g (3½oz) skinless, boneless smoked
    haddock, cut into bitesize pieces
2 spring onions (scallions), finely sliced,
    plus extra to serve
**about 200g (7oz) Tomato Baked Rice
    (see page 22)**
1 chicken or vegetable stock cube
a small knob of unsalted butter (optional)
2 hard-boiled eggs, peeled and halved
a few coriander (cilantro) leaves, to serve (optional)

01 Pour the oil into a large frying pan over a medium-high heat.

02 When hot, add the smoked haddock and spring onions (scallions), reduce the heat a little, and fry for 2-3 minutes to soften.

03 Add the Tomato Baked Rice along with 100ml (3½fl oz) of water, the crumbled stock cube and the butter (if using), then bring to the simmer, stir well and leave to cook for a further 2-3 minutes, until the haddock is cooked through.

04 Tip the kedgeree into a serving bowl and top with the hard-boiled eggs. Serve with a final flourish of spring onions and some coriander (cilantro) leaves, too, if you like.

ULTIMATE BROCCOLI SUB

This remix has got your back when you can't focus on making anything more complicated for supper than a sandwich – those reserved stems of blanched broccoli are about to come into their own. For some extra texture, you could add some crispy fried onions if you have them, or, to liven things up, a drizzle of chilli sauce. If you don't have feta, cheddar or gouda would work well.

Serves 2   15 minutes

8 stems of blanched longstem broccoli from Longstem Broccoli with Red Pepper Hummus (see page 23)
2 tablespoons malt vinegar (or any vinegar you have)
2 tablespoons wholegrain mustard (or spicy condiment of choice)
6 tablespoons red pepper hummus from Longstem Broccoli with Red Pepper Hummus
2 soft baguette rolls, sliced open, but left attached
6 mint leaves, sliced into thin strips
40g (1¼oz) feta cheese, crumbled

01 Preheat the grill (broiler) to medium-high. Place the broccoli in a mixing bowl and add the vinegar and mustard, tossing gently to coat. Set aside.

02 Place 3 tablespoons of the red pepper hummus on to the cut side of the bottom of each roll, spreading it out to create a thin layer.

03 Scatter over the mint strips, then place 4 broccoli stems into each roll, alternating the direction of the stalks and heads so that the subs will close evenly and are nicely balanced.

04 Sprinkle over the crumbled cheese, then place the subs on to a baking sheet, keeping them hinged open for now. Place them under the grill for 2-3 minutes, until the cheese is beginning to melt. Remove from the grill and close the lids to sandwich. Serve straight away.

PEACH MELBA
SUNDAE

*I always crave something sweet at the end of a
meal and have a habit of indulging. Sometimes,
I just need a square of chocolate or a deliciously
ripe plum, but if I've made a tart earlier in the
week, a couple of reserved spoonfuls of the fruit
filling served with vanilla ice cream and leftover
sauce makes a perfect sundae – perfect enough to
appease my inner child, and also to make my
adult self proud should I have guests.*

Serves 2   10 minutes

4 scoops of vanilla ice cream (or as much as you
    like)
**stewed peaches and raspberry sauce from
    Peach Melba Tart (see page 24)**

01 Simply put 2 scoops of vanilla ice cream into
each serving dish and top with the leftover stewed
peaches and raspberry sauce to create a sundae.

Confit Jerusalem Artichoke Soup *with* Pickled Mushroom Toast

Serves 4–6

1 hour

250g (9oz) unsalted butter

300g (10oz) Jerusalem artichokes, peeled and sliced into 1cm (½in) rounds

1 red onion, chopped

6 garlic cloves, crushed

400ml (14fl oz) vegetable stock

salt and freshly ground black pepper

For the pickled mushrooms

50ml (1¾fl oz) sherry vinegar

1 teaspoon caster (superfine) sugar

20g (¾oz) dried wild mushrooms

For the toast

4 slices of sourdough

60g (1oz) cheddar or pecorino, grated

01 First, make the pickled mushrooms. Place the vinegar and sugar in a small saucepan with 3 tablespoons of water over a high heat. Bring to a boil, then boil for 1 minute. Tip the dried mushrooms into a heatproof jar and pour over the hot liquid. Leave to steep like this for 10 minutes, or while you make the soup.

02 For the soup, melt the butter in a frying pan over a low heat. Add the artichokes, onion and garlic and cook gently for 30–40 minutes, stirring occasionally to make sure the artichoke slices are submerged in the butter, until completely soft with a beautiful, golden hue. Turn off the heat.

03 Place a sieve over a jug and drain the artichokes, catching the butter in the jug. ***To make the Jerusalem Artichoke and Broccoli Risotto (see page 42), pour the butter into an ice-cube tray and cover. Refrigerate it for up to 4 days, or freeze for up to 1 month (defrost before using).***

04 Put the artichokes back into the pan, place over a medium–low heat, and pour in the vegetable stock. Season with salt and pepper and bring the mixture to a simmer, then turn off the heat and use a hand-held stick blender to blitz the liquid until it is completely smooth. ***To make the Jerusalem Artichoke and Broccoli Risotto, pour 150ml (5fl oz) of the soup into an airtight container. Refrigerate for up to 4 days, or freeze it for up to 1 month (defrost before using).*** Keep the remaining soup warm while you make the toast.

05 Preheat the grill (broiler) to high. Place the sourdough on a baking tray and toast until golden on one side. Remove the tray from the grill, turn over the slices and top each with 2 or 3 of the pickled mushrooms. Sprinkle over the cheese, then place the laden toast back under the grill until the cheese is melted and lightly caramelized around the edges. Halve the slices to serve alongside bowls of the soup.

Spinach *and* Feta Custard Pie

Serves 4–6

1 hour 15 minutes

1 egg

1 egg yolk

1 tablespoon caster (superfine) sugar

1 tablespoon cornflour (corn starch)

375ml (13fl oz) whole milk

½ teaspoon freshly ground black pepper,
    plus extra to season

a generous bunch of thyme sprigs

a pinch of salt, plus extra to season

60g (2oz) fine semolina

45g (1½oz) unsalted butter, plus extra
    (melted) for brushing

3 tablespoons flavourless oil

2 small onions, chopped

1 teaspoon nigella seeds, plus extra
    for sprinkling

250g (9oz) spinach leaves

200g (7oz) feta

3 large sheets of filo pastry

3 tablespoons sesame seeds

01 Place the egg, egg yolk, sugar and cornflour (corn starch) into a mixing bowl and whisk together until frothy. Set aside.

02 Place the milk into a medium saucepan over a medium heat. Add the black pepper, thyme sprigs and the pinch of salt and bring to a boil.

03 Once the milk is boiling, remove the thyme from the pan using a fork, then pour the hot milk into the egg mixture, whisking continuously for 1–2 minutes to form a custard.

04 Pour the custard back into the pan and place over a low heat. Little by little, add the semolina, whisking to combine between each addition. Keep whisking until the mixture is thick enough to come away from the bottom of the pan. Then, continue to stir for 1–2 minutes, until the custard is thick and has the consistency of mashed potato.

05 Remove the pan from the heat and add the butter, stirring until it is completely melted and combined. Set aside and allow the custard to cool.

06 Meanwhile, heat the oil in a large frying pan over a high heat. When hot, add the onions and season with salt and pepper. Fry for 8–10 minutes, until golden brown, then add the nigella seeds and fry for a further 1–2 minutes. Tip the contents of the pan on to a plate and set aside.

07 Put the pan back on the heat. Add the spinach and about 100ml (3½fl oz) of water, stirring occasionally to make sure the spinach doesn't stick. Cook for about 5–10 minutes, until the leaves are fully wilted and the water has evaporated.

08 Stir in half the cooked onion mixture and set aside for 10 minutes to cool. (Alternatively, you can make the filling the day before, if you like.) ***To make the Semolina Chips (see page 43), transfer 3 tablespoons of the remaining onion mixture to an airtight container. Refrigerate for up to 3 days.***

09 Add the remaining onion mixture to the custard. Add the feta and stir to combine and season with salt and pepper. Set aside again.

10 Once the filling has cooled for 10 minutes, lay out 1 sheet of filo pastry, with the longest edge closest to you. Brush the whole sheet with a thin layer of melted butter, then add another sheet of filo and brush again with butter. Add the final sheet of pastry. Spoon the custard into the middle, smoothing it out into a square, leaving at least a 3cm (1¼in) border around the edges. Add the spinach mixture on top, spreading it out evenly. Fold the pastry edge closest to you up and over the filling and fold down the edge farthest from you. Then, fold in the two sides, so that the filling is fully encased.

11 Lightly butter a baking tray or line a baking tray with greaseproof paper. Carefully flip the tart over so that the folded sides are underneath and transfer it to the baking tray. Brush the top of the pie with melted butter and sprinkle over the sesame seeds and extra nigella seeds. Bake for 20–25 minutes, until golden.

"Everything Seasoning" Potatoes

Serves 4–6

45 minutes

4 large potatoes, peeled and cut into
    3cm (1¼in) cubes
boiling water from a kettle
4 tablespoons flavourless oil
salt and freshly ground black pepper

For the Everything Seasoning

6 teaspoons poppy seeds
4 teaspoons dried garlic flakes
4 teaspoons crispy fried onions
2 teaspoons black sesame seeds, toasted
    in a dry pan
2 teaspoons white sesame seeds, toasted
    in a dry pan
2 teaspoons nigella seeds

For the sweet chilli cream cheese

1 roasted red (bell) pepper, from a jar
3 teaspoons chilli oil
1 tablespoon maple syrup
200g (7oz) full-fat cream cheese

01 Preheat the oven to 230°C (210°C fan/450°F/Gas 8).

02 Place the potatoes in a medium saucepan with a generous seasoning of salt. Pour in boiling water to cover, place the pan over a high heat and boil the potatoes for 10 minutes, until tender. Drain in a colander and leave to steam off for 5 minutes.

03 In the meantime, combine all the ingredients for the Everything Seasoning and stir well. ***This will make enough seasoning also for the Corned Beef Hash (see page 44). Transfer the seasoning to an airtight container and store for up to 2 weeks.***

04 Pour the oil into a baking tray, then tip in the potatoes. Stir to coat, then roast for 25–30 minutes, until crispy.

05 Meanwhile, make the sweet chilli cream cheese. Place the red (bell) pepper in a food processor along with the chilli oil and maple syrup and pulse until the pepper is chopped into small pieces. Add the cream cheese and pulse again to combine. ***To make the Red Pepper and Cream Cheese Pasta (see page 44), place half the mixture into an airtight container. Refrigerate for up to 2 days.***

06 Spread out the remaining cream cheese mixture on to a serving plate. ***To make the Corned Beef Hash, place a generous handful of the potatoes into an airtight container. Refrigerate them for up to 2 days.*** Spoon the remaining crispy potatoes on top of the cream cheese mixture and sprinkle with a couple of tablespoons of the Everything Seasoning.

Tonka Bean Tres Leches Cake *with* Roasted Strawberries

Serves 8–10

1 hour 30 minutes, plus chilling

200g (7oz) salted butter, softened, plus
  extra for greasing
3 eggs, separated
200g (7oz/scant 1 cup) caster (superfine)
  sugar, divided equally into two
    100g (3½oz/scant ½ cup) portions
1 tonka bean, grated, or 1 tablespoon
  vanilla paste
½ teaspoon almond extract
1 teaspoon ground cinnamon
1 teaspoon baking powder
200g (7oz/1⅓ cups) plain (all-purpose) flour
200ml (7fl oz) whole milk
1 x 397g can of condensed milk
1 x 410g can of evaporated milk

For the roasted strawberries
200g (7oz) strawberries, hulled
100g (3½oz/scant ½ cup) caster (superfine)
  sugar

01 Preheat the oven to 200°C (180°C fan/400°F/Gas 6).

02 Grease a 20cm (8in) cake tin with butter and line it (bottom and sides) with greaseproof paper.

03 Place the egg whites in a large, clean bowl and whisk with an electric hand whisk to form soft peaks. One third at a time, add one portion of the sugar, whisking well between each addition, until you have a stiff meringue.

04 Tip the remaining portion of sugar into a separate large bowl. Add the butter, the egg yolks, the grated tonka bean or the vanilla paste, the almond extract and the cinnamon. Using an electric hand mixer, beat the mixture together until it is creamy and light.

05 Mix the baking powder into the flour, then add half the flour mixture and 50ml (1¾fl oz) of the milk to the bowl with the egg-yolk mixture and beat until fully incorporated. Add the remainder of the flour mixture and another 50ml (1¾fl oz) of the milk and beat again until everything is mixed together to form a batter.

06 One third at a time, fold the meringue into the batter until it is fully incorporated with no flecks of white.

07 Pour the batter into the prepared cake tin and place it in the centre of the oven to bake for 35–40 minutes, until a wooden skewer inserted into the centre comes out clean. (If it's not quite ready, pop it back in the oven for 5 minutes, then test again.) Remove the cake from the oven (but leave the oven on) and leave to cool in the tin while you make the roasted strawberries.

08 Place the hulled strawberries into a baking tray lined with greaseproof paper and sprinkle with the sugar. Roast for 15–20 minutes, until the strawberries are softened and the sugar has melted. Transfer the strawberries, and any cooking juices in the tray, to a heatproof bowl ready for later. ***To make the Vietnamese Coffee (see page 46), measure 2 tablespoons each of the condensed milk and the evaporated milk into an airtight container and combine. Refrigerate the mixture for up to 5 days.***

09 In a mixing bowl, combine the remaining condensed milk, evaporated milk and whole milk. Once the cake has slightly cooled, pour the mixture over the cake and refrigerate for 2 hours. Spoon some of the strawberries and their cooking juices over each slice of cake, to serve.

JERUSALEM ARTICHOKE AND BROCCOLI RISOTTO

The artichoke butter left over from the confit artichokes is truly game changing – it adds smoky, savoury depth to this risotto (and has the same effect on a cheese toastie). Adding the soup at the end gives the risotto the silkiest of textures. I just wish I could buy artichokes more often – this is definitely a recipe I could eat every week.

Serves 2–3   30 minutes

10g (¼oz) dried mixed mushrooms
400ml (14fl oz) boiling water from a kettle
2 tablespoons melted butter from Confit
    Jerusalem Artichoke Soup with Pickled
    Mushroom Toast (see page 32)
120g (4¼oz) arborio risotto rice
5 longstem broccoli, stalks chopped into
    2cm (¾in) pieces, florets separated and
    chopped
150ml (5fl oz) Confit Jerusalem Artichoke Soup
salt and freshly ground black pepper
30g (1oz) parmesan or pecorino, grated,
    to serve

01 Place the dried mushrooms in a heatproof jug and pour over the boiling water. Leave to stand for 5 minutes to rehydrate the mushrooms and infuse the water. Drain the mushrooms, reserving the soaking liquid, and set both aside.

02 Melt the butter in a large frying pan over a medium–high heat. Add the rice and stir to coat. Cook for 4 minutes, until the rice begins to look slightly opaque.

03 Pour in a quarter of the mushroom soaking liquid, being careful as it may splash slightly. Stir, then leave for 2–3 minutes, until all of the liquid is absorbed. Continue to add the soaking liquid, a little at a time, stirring and allowing the rice to absorb it before adding more.

04 When you have the last quarter of the soaking liquid left, add the chopped broccoli stalks and florets to the risotto, then the remaining soaking liquid. Allow the rice to absorb the liquid, so that the grains are tender and the broccoli is cooked.

05 Add the soup, stir, and heat through until hot, seasoning well with salt and pepper.

06 Ladle the risotto equally into two or three large bowls and serve straight away, sprinkled with the grated cheese.

SEMOLINA CHIPS

*Dipped into some lemony mayonnaise, these
semolina chips are a meal in themselves. Don't be
put off by the cooking and chilling time – apart
from a bit of mixing and frying, there's really very
little to do. This recipe is a great way to use up a
bag of semolina (and a good reason to have one).*

Serves 2   30 minutes, plus chilling

1 tablespoon flavourless oil, plus 300ml (10fl oz)
      for deep frying
**3 tablespoons of the onion mixture from Spinach
      and Feta Custard Pie (see page 34)**
2 garlic cloves, finely chopped
6 thyme sprigs, leaves picked
400ml (14fl oz) vegetable stock
180g (6¼oz) fine semolina
45g (1½oz) mature cheddar, grated,
      or crumbled feta
salt and freshly ground black pepper

01 Heat the tablespoon of oil in a deep frying
pan over a high heat. When hot, add the onion
mixture, garlic and thyme and fry for 2–3 minutes,
until the onion begins to turn lightly golden around
the edges.

02 Pour in the stock. Little by little, add the
semolina, stirring continuously to avoid any
lumps. When the mixture is the consistency of
mashed potato (about 2–3 minutes), remove it
from the heat, season with salt and pepper and
stir in the cheese.

03 Line the bottom of a 20cm (8in) square cake
tin with greaseproof paper. Spoon in the semolina
mixture, flattening and smoothing the top. Allow to
cool, then refrigerate for about 30 minutes to firm
up. Once the mixture has cooled and is firm, cut it
into large rectangles.

04 Heat the 300ml (10fl oz) of oil in a deep frying
pan over a medium–high heat until it reaches
170°C (340°F) on a cooking thermometer (or a
small amount of the semolina mixture sizzles
as soon as it hits the oil). Deep-fry the chips for
1–2 minutes on each side, until golden, then
remove from the oil and drain on kitchen paper
before serving. (Alternatively, cook them in an
airfryer for 10 minutes with 1 tablespoon of oil.)

RED PEPPER AND CREAM CHEESE PASTA

Serves 2   15 minutes

200g (7oz) dried pasta of your choice
2 tablespoons flavourless oil
1 onion, chopped
1 x 340g can of sweetcorn, drained
**6 tablespoons sweet chilli cream cheese
    from the "Everything Seasoning" Potatoes
    (see page 38)**
4 pitted black olives, finely chopped (optional)
a few basil leaves (optional)
salt

<u>01</u> Bring a large saucepan of salted water to a boil. Add the pasta and cook according to the packet instructions, until al dente.

<u>02</u> Meanwhile, heat the oil in a frying pan over a medium–high heat. Add the onion and the sweetcorn and fry for 4–5 minutes, until the onion begins to brown.

<u>03</u> Once the pasta is almost cooked, take a ladleful of the pasta cooking water and add it to the pan with the onion, then stir in the sweet chilli cream cheese and allow the sauce to bubble away.

<u>04</u> Drain the cooked pasta and tip it into the pan with the sauce. Stir to coat, then serve the pasta in bowls with the chopped olives and basil on top, if you wish.

CORNED BEEF HASH

Serves 2   20 minutes

2 tablespoons flavourless oil, plus extra
    for the eggs
1 onion, sliced into half moons
1 head of spring greens, thinly sliced
1 x 340g can of corned beef, cut into 3cm (1½in)
    cubes
**a handful of "Everything Seasoning" Potatoes
    (see page 38)**
**1 tablespoon everything seasoning from
    "Everything Seasoning" Potatoes**
2 eggs
salt and freshly ground black pepper
finely chopped chives, to serve (optional)

<u>01</u> Heat the oil in a large frying pan over a high heat. When hot, add the onion and the spring greens and fry for about 3–4 minutes, until the onion has lightly browned and the greens have wilted.

<u>02</u> Add 1 tablespoon of water and season with a little salt, then fry for a further 5–6 minutes, until all of the water has evaporated.

<u>03</u> Add the corned beef cubes to the pan along with the potatoes and seasoning and cook for a further 5–6 minutes, until the corned beef is beginning to caramelize around the edges and is hot through.

<u>04</u> Divide the corned beef hash between two warmed plates and set aside.

<u>05</u> Place the pan back over a high heat, add a small glug of oil and, when hot, crack the eggs into the pan. Fry them to your liking, then serve them on top of the hash, seasoned with salt and pepper and sprinkled with chives, if you wish.

VIETNAMESE COFFEE

I went through a stage of being absolutely obsessed with coffee and even trained to be a barista for a short while. It still blows my mind how many different coffee varieties there are and how many ways to drink them. To me, there is something particularly special about Vietnamese coffee and I always make sure, if I'm using condensed milk for another recipe, I leave some spare to make myself this.

Serves 2   10 minutes

**4 tablespoons condensed and evaporated milk
    mixture from Tonka Bean Tres Leches Cake
    (see page 40)**
4 teaspoons dark roast espresso powder

01 Place 2 tablespoons of the milk mixture into a heatproof glass and stir to combine. Do the same in a second glass.

02 Place 2 teaspoons of espresso powder into a Vietnamese coffee maker and make the coffee according to the coffee-maker instructions, allowing the coffee to drip through into one of the glasses. Repeat for the remaining powder and second glass of milk. Serve straight away.

Alternatively, make any type of black coffee you have available and add it to the glasses with the milk, stirring well before serving.

Scallops
with Spring
Onion Oil

Serves 2

35 minutes

6 large, fresh scallops, shelled

2 teaspoons Maggi's liquid seasoning
   (or other umami-rich liquid bouillon)
   or dark soy sauce

1 teaspoon dried chilli flakes

sea salt

For the spring onion oil

200ml (7fl oz) flavourless oil

6 small banana shallots, halved lengthways

6 spring onions (scallions), sliced into
   3cm (1¼in) pieces

For the spring onion mayonnaise

1 egg yolk

1 tablespoon white vinegar

1 teaspoon sesame oil

01 First, make the spring onion oil. Place the oil in a large frying pan over a low heat. When the oil is just hot, place the shallots into the pan and allow to cook gently for 6–8 minutes, until they begin to brown. Turn off the heat. Remove the shallots from the pan and transfer them into a sterilized jar or heatproof container.

02 Return the pan to a low heat and add the spring onions (scallions). Cook for 6–8 minutes, until the spring onions begin to soften. Set aside 6 pieces, then transfer the remainder to the jar with the shallots.

03 Measure out 150ml (5fl oz) of the oil and set aside. ***To make the Spring Onion Oil and Brown Sugar Noodles (see page 56), very carefully pour the remaining oil into the jar with the shallots and spring onions and seal with the lid. Refrigerate for up to 1 month.***

04 Make the spring onion mayonnaise. Add the egg yolk and vinegar to a food processor and blend together. Then, slowly add the sesame oil and 100ml (3½fl oz) of the reserved spring onion oil, until the mixture begins to thicken to a mayonnaise consistency. Transfer to a bowl, cover and set aside in the fridge until needed.

05 Using a sharp knife, make diagonal cuts across the top of each scallop, being careful not to slice all the way through (this step isn't essential – but it does make the scallops look lovely).

06 Heat the remaining reserved spring onion oil in a frying pan over a medium–high heat. When hot, place the scallops into the pan, cut side down, and add the reserved 6 pieces of spring onion. Cook the scallops for 2–3 minutes, until deeply golden brown on the underside, then turn them over and cook for 1 minute more, until golden and cooked through. Remove from the pan.

07 To serve, place 3 tablespoons of the spring onion mayonnaise on each plate (or divide the mayo into 6 cleaned scallop shells) and top each mayo "puddle" with a scallop. Season with sea salt, then sprinkle over a little liquid seasoning or soy sauce and the chilli flakes. Top each scallop with a piece of fried spring onion.

Herbed
Monkfish

Serves 2

35 minutes

1 head of garlic, sliced in half widthways

4 slices of bread or 300g (10oz) fresh
  breadcrumbs

a small bunch of mint, leaves picked
  and roughly chopped

a small bunch of flat-leaf parsley, leaves
  picked and roughly chopped

a small bunch of dill, feathery leaves picked
  and roughly chopped

1 egg

100ml (3½fl oz) whole milk

100g (3½oz) plain (all-purpose) flour

2 monkfish fillets (about 200g/7oz each)

120ml (4fl oz) flavourless oil

2 tablespoons malt vinegar

juice of 1 lemon, plus extra wedges
  (optional) to serve

90g (3oz) mayonnaise

sea salt

01 Remove 4 pieces of garlic clove from the top
half of the sliced garlic head.

02 Place the slices of bread or the breadcrumbs in
a food processor and add the 4 pieces of garlic clove
along with the herbs. Pulse to a fine, herby breadcrumb.
*__To make the Garlic Breadcrumb and Prawn Spaghetti
(see page 57), transfer 6 tablespoons to an airtight
container. Store at room temperature for up to 4 days,
or freeze for up to 1 month (use from frozen).__*

03 Beat the egg and milk together in a wide bowl. Tip
the flour on to a plate. Tip the remaining breadcrumbs
into a baking tray. Dip each fish fillet fully in the flour,
then in the egg mixture, then lay each into the
breadcrumbs and turn to coat both sides. Set aside.

04 Heat the oil in a large frying pan over a medium–
high heat. Place both halves of the head of garlic,
cut sides down, into the pan and leave for 2–3 minutes
while the oil heats up.

05 When the oil is hot, place both of the breaded
fish fillets into the pan and cook on each side for
6–8 minutes, until the breadcrumbs are golden and
crispy and the fish is cooked through. Set aside and
keep warm.

06 Once the garlic is deeply browned, remove it from
the pan and, once it's cool enough to handle, squeeze
the base to pop out the toasted cloves. Place these in a
food processor and pulse to form a paste. Add the malt
vinegar and the lemon juice and stir to combine. Mix this
mixture into the mayonnaise and season with sea salt.
Serve alongside the fish, along with extra wedges of
lemon for squeezing over, if you wish.

Greens *with* Chilli and Ginger

Serves 2

15 minutes

3 tablespoons flavourless oil

1 head of spring greens or 1 savoy
    cabbage, thinly sliced

8 Brussels sprouts, thinly sliced

1 red chilli, deseeded and finely chopped

1 green chilli, deseeded and finely chopped

5 spring onions (scallions), thinly sliced

2 tablespoons garlic paste

1½ tablespoons ginger paste

a large handful of basil, leaves picked
    and roughly chopped

3 tablespoons light soy sauce

01 Heat the oil in a large frying pan over a high heat.
Add the greens or cabbage and sprouts and fry for about
5–6 minutes, until the slices start to smell slightly sweet
and aromatic (it's okay if some pieces start to brown
slightly – this adds a delicious smoky flavour).

02 Add the chillies, spring onions (scallions), and garlic
and ginger pastes and fry for a further 1–2 minutes,
then add the basil and soy sauce. Mix well and simmer
for 2 minutes, until the basil leaves have wilted. **_To make
the Okonomiyaki-ish Pancakes (see page 58), place
half the greens mixture in an airtight container.
Refrigerate for up to 3 days._** Serve the remaining
greens straight away.

Pineapple Donuts *with* Coconut Kaya Jam

Makes about 10

45 minutes

For the coconut kaya jam

1 x 400g can of full-fat coconut milk

3 large eggs

1 egg yolk

200g (7oz/scant 1 cup) golden caster (superfine) sugar

4 dried pandan leaves or two 3cm (1¼in) pieces of fresh pandan leaf

about 100ml (3½fl oz) boiling water from a kettle

70g (2¼oz/½ cup) coarsely grated palm sugar

For the sugar coating

150g (5½oz/⅔ cup) caster (superfine) sugar

1 teaspoon ground cinnamon

¼ teaspoon grated nutmeg

¼ teaspoon fine salt

For the pineapple donuts

150g (5½oz/1 cup) self-raising flour

80g (2¾oz/⅓ cup) caster (superfine) sugar

½ teaspoon ground cinnamon

¼ teaspoon grated nutmeg

200g (7oz) fresh pineapple flesh, cut into 3cm (1¼in) chunks (or use canned chunks)

90ml (3fl oz) whole milk

1 egg

500ml (16fl oz) flavourless oil, for deep frying

01 Make the coconut kaya jam. Place the coconut milk, eggs and egg yolk into a mixing bowl with the golden caster (superfine) sugar and whisk together.

02 Place the pandan leaves or pieces into a small bowl and cover with the boiling water, making sure that the leaves are completely submerged. Leave for 10 minutes to infuse.

03 Place the palm sugar into a small saucepan over a medium–low heat. Strain the water from the pandan leaves into the pan (reserve the leaves), stir well, then bring to a boil to dissolve the sugar. Turn off the heat.

04 Transfer the coconut-milk mixture and the pandan leaves into a large saucepan over a low heat, whisking continuously for about 10–15 minutes, until the mixture has thickened to the consistency of a soft lemon curd.

05 Add the hot palm sugar syrup to the pan and heat, still whisking, for a further 1–2 minutes to incorporate. Remove the jam from the heat and transfer it to a sterilized container. Set aside for later.

06 Make the sugar coating by simply combining all the ingredients in a large mixing bowl. Set aside.

07 Make the pineapple donuts. Combine the dry ingredients in a large mixing bowl, then stir through the pineapple.

08 Whisk together the milk and egg in a separate bowl, then add the mixture to the dry ingredients, stirring well to make a thick batter.

09 Pour the oil into a deep, heavy-based saucepan and heat to 170°C (340°F), or until a drop of batter sizzles as it hits the oil. (Alternatively, use a deep-fat fryer.)

10 To make the donuts, take 1 tablespoon of the batter and use another spoon to push it into the hot oil, being careful not to splash yourself. Repeat until you're cooking 5 donuts at a time, stirring them occasionally, for about 3–4 minutes, until evenly browned all over.

11 Using a slotted spoon, remove the donuts from the pan and drop them into the bowl with the flavoured sugar, tossing to coat. Repeat until you've used up all the batter (about 10 donuts).

12 Transfer the donuts to serving bowls or plates. ***To make the Kaya Toast (see page 60), reserve 4 tablespoons of the coconut kaya jam in a sterilized container.*** Remove the pandan leaves and serve the remaining jam alongside the donuts for dipping.

SPRING ONION OIL AND BROWN SUGAR NOODLES

If you can get your hands on palm sugar, I really recommend it for this recipe – its nutty sweetness is so addictive. Paired with the spring onion oil, it creates noodles that are glossy and rich. Maggi's seasoning – an umami-rich liquid seasoning – is a kitchen staple for me. A little goes a long way.

Serves 2-3   10 minutes

4 tablespoons spring onion oil (including the pieces) from Scallops with Spring Onion Oil (see page 48)
3 teaspoons palm sugar or light brown soft sugar
3 tablespoons light soy sauce
1 teaspoon dried chilli flakes (optional)
400g (14oz) fresh egg noodles
1 teaspoon Maggi's liquid seasoning (or other umami-rich liquid bouillon)
2 spring onions (scallions), thinly sliced (optional), to serve

01 Tip the spring onion oil and pieces into a large frying pan or wok and place over a high heat.

02 Spoon in the sugar and allow it to melt for 2-3 minutes, then add the soy sauce and chilli flakes, stirring quickly to mix them together.

03 Tear apart the noodles and place them into the pan, using a wooden spoon to stir and cover them in the sauce. Cook for 2-3 minutes, then tip them into serving bowls, sprinkle in the seasoning and scatter over the sliced spring onions (scallions), if using, and serve.

GARLIC BREADCRUMB AND PRAWN SPAGHETTI

During the weeks when I'm feeling budget conscious, garlic breadcrumb spaghetti is a great friend. The prawns are delicious, but you could make the recipe even more cost-effective by using a can of anchovies in their place, or simply omitting them altogether. Either way, this simple and elegant supper feels anything but budget.

Serves 2   15 minutes

6 tablespoons herby breadcrumbs from Herbed Monkfish (see page 50)
140g (5oz) dried spaghetti, or other pasta of choice
1 tablespoon unsalted butter
2 garlic cloves, thinly sliced
1 teaspoon freshly ground black pepper
100g (3½oz) fresh or frozen peeled prawns (shrimp)
salt

01 First, bake the breadcrumbs. Preheat the oven to 200°C (180°C fan/400°F/Gas 4). Scatter the breadcrumbs (from frozen is fine) over a baking tray and bake for 10 minutes, until golden and crispy. Remove from the oven and set aside.

02 Bring a large saucepan of salted water to a boil. Add the pasta and cook according to the packet instructions, until al dente.

03 Meanwhile, melt the butter in a medium frying pan over a medium–high heat. Add the garlic and black pepper. Reduce the heat to medium and cook for 4–5 minutes, until the garlic begins to brown and smell aromatic.

04 Add the prawns (shrimp), then add a ladleful of the pasta cooking water. Cook for 3–4 minutes, until the liquid is reduced by half, and silky. Add 1 tablespoon of the breadcrumbs and stir to thicken the sauce.

05 Drain the pasta and transfer it to the pan with the sauce, mixing well to coat.

06 Divide the pasta between two serving bowls and sprinkle over the remaining breadcrumbs to serve.

OKONOMIYAKI-ISH PANCAKES

The garlic and soy that are already in the Greens with Chilli and Ginger elevate this remix to something really special – but you can make a version with any leftover leafy greens. My first ever okonomiyaki pancake was in London's Brixton market – it was served with bonito flakes (wafer-like dried fish pieces) and I was in awe of how much deep umami flavour was held in their paper thinness. It was one of those precious world-food moments to cherish.

Serves 2   25 minutes

½ **quantity of Greens with Chilli and Ginger (see page 51)**
2 eggs, lightly beaten
100ml (3½fl oz) warm water
100g (3½oz) frozen peas
1 teaspoon flavourless oil

TO SERVE
a generous drizzle of mayonnaise
a generous drizzle of bulldog sauce
     or brown sauce
2 spring onions (scallions), sliced (optional)

<u>01</u> Tip the greens into a large mixing bowl along with the eggs, water and frozen peas. Use a fork to mix well for about 2–3 minutes, until the eggs are properly broken up and everything is combined.

<u>02</u> Heat the oil in a non-stick frying pan over a medium-high heat. Pour in half the egg mixture and reduce the heat to medium-low. Cook the omelette for 3 minutes, then place a lid on the pan and cook for a further 5–6 minutes, until the omelette is firm on top when you remove the lid.

<u>03</u> Turn off the heat and grab a large plate. Place the plate on top of the pan and carefully invert the omelette on to it. Keep warm while you make the second omelette.

<u>04</u> To serve, top each omelette with generous drizzles of mayonnaise and bulldog or brown sauce, and a scattering of spring onions (scallions), if you wish.

KAYA TOAST

Kaya jam has a deep, caramelized coconut flavour mixed with the rich, aromatic – almost vanilla-like – scent of pandan. It pairs so well with salted butter. This recipe is like the grown-up version of the jam on toast I used to have as a kid. And, truth be told, I'd happily dispense with the toast – I love dipping wedges of apple into a dollop of the jam for a sweet kick at the end of a meal.

Serves 2   20–30 minutes

2 tablespoons salted butter, plus 2 teaspoons
    for frying
4 slices of thick-cut sourdough, crusts removed
**4 tablespoons coconut kaya jam from the
    Pineapple Donuts with Coconut Kaya Jam
    (see page 54)**

01 Butter one side of each slice of the sourdough. Spread a layer of the kaya jam on each slice, then sandwich the slices together to make 2 sandwiches.

02 Melt 1 teaspoon of butter in a frying pan over a medium heat. When hot, place 1 sandwich into the pan. Fry for 4–5 minutes on each side, until browned all over. Remove the sandwich from the pan, cut in half and serve.

03 Repeat for the other sandwich.

Autumn

Autumn has to be my favourite time of the year – I unashamedly turn into a chai-latte-drinking, green-jumper-wearing, cosy-library-craving person. My memories of autumn largely also involve my sister. She would save up some of her lunch money from the week and we would make the pilgrimage into Newcastle, where she would buy me a hot chocolate dusted with cinnamon, and a slice of cake – catering to the sweet tooth that I still have. When we got home, if we were very lucky, our mam would have made us a curry – from a jar, always, but we thought it was the height of culinary sophistication. All of those happy childhood memories of autumn are reflected in this chapter – with warming spices and decadent sweetness in every menu (but no jarred sauces).

All creations great and small – this menu features delicious little prawns and a generous rib of beef. I'm serving two, but if there were ever a "very" dinner party menu, it's this (if you don't make the remixes, it will serve more). I love making Chinese dumplings (filling and wrapping is so therapeutic) – I must have made hundreds over the years – and I think these Prawn and Scallop ones are my best to date. I first tasted the Thai flavour of gra prow stir-fries (all lemongrass, chilli, Thai basil, and ginger) at my friend Siri's stall in Camden Market, London. I love recreating it. Here, it comes with Salt and Pepper Potatoes – spicy, sweet, utterly moreish – on the side. You'll find a sophisticated kind of chocolate tart for dessert, making the most of delicious autumn pears (sophisticated, yes, but the Oreo cookies in the base bring glee to my inner child).

Like I say, autumn to me is more reminiscent of home than any other season, and the second menu – **Northern (street)lights, the taste of home** – is all that. I love the hearty foods of the North. For the recipe that boasts the most return, possibly in the whole book, make the Honey and Bay Roasted Ham – one large ham gives enough for four meals, each as delicious as the next. Cheddar and Chive Flat Breads with Roasted Tomatoes brings a flavour combination that reminds me of my mum's special cheese on toast – ramped up a few notches by roasting the tomatoes and adding chives. Roasting swede adds extra layers, too, to this humble root vegetable, certainly compared with the mash of my youth (I still love mashed swede, but this version is better). In a menu that celebrates where I'm from, I absolutely had to have tea and cake for dessert – there's nothing more northern than a good cup of tea. The Earl Grey flavour in the custard is amazing – even just the smell is out of this world. The recipe makes 12 cakes for a dinner for four people, because, well, why make cakes if there aren't any extra for the week?

Finally, **An abundance of spice**. Making your own samosa dough is easy and just so worth it (you absolutely reserve the right to stash a couple of samosas away in the fridge for later). I look forward to meals like the Paneer, Cashew and Green Lentil Curry – the kind of dish that makes a house a home – all week. Roasted sweet potatoes with chutneys and puffed rice make the perfect side, the sweet flavours and silky textures bringing the curry to life. Brick Lane in Shoreditch, London, is packed with gorgeous Indian shops with rows of brightly coloured sweets. I remember taking my best friend Ryan to my favourite and asking the man for a portion of *jalebi*, a crispy fritter soaked in saffron syrup. He gave us a whole box for free so that Ryan could experience the magic. I've never forgotten his kindness and always make the trip to his shop when I'm in east London. When I'm not, I make my own and save the leftover spiced syrup to make chai lattes in the week – wrapped up in my autumnal green jumper, of course.

Autumn

Prawn *and* Scallop Dumplings

Serves 2

35 minutes

250g (9oz) fresh, peeled prawns (shrimp)

250g (9oz) small shelled scallops

a small handful of chives, chopped

2 spring onions (scallions), finely sliced

3 tablespoons light soy sauce

2 tablespoons caster (superfine) sugar

1 tablespoon sesame oil, plus ½ teaspoon
    for the filling

¼ teaspoon ground white pepper

½ napa cabbage, finely chopped

1 leek, finely chopped

10 dumpling pastry skins

2 tablespoons flavourless oil

salt

equal parts light soy sauce and malt vinegar
    mixed with slivers of 1cm (½in) piece
    of peeled fresh ginger, for dipping,
    to serve

01 Make a seafood paste. Put the prawns (shrimp), scallops, chives, spring onions (scallions), 2 tablespoons of the soy sauce, and all the sugar, sesame oil and white pepper into a food processor. Blitz to a coarse paste. Add a sprinkle of salt to season and stir well to combine. *To make the Prawn Toast (see page 76), reserve 6 tablespoons of the seafood paste in an airtight container. Refrigerate for up to 2 days.*

02 Tip the remaining paste into a large mixing bowl and add the cabbage and leek. Mix well to combine, then add the remaining tablespoon of soy sauce and the ½ teaspoon of sesame oil and mix well again.

03 Take a dumpling pastry skin in the palm of your hand and place 1 teaspoon of the mixture into the middle – don't be tempted to overfill. Dip your finger in a bowl of water and run it around the edge of half the pastry circle. Gently fold the pastry over the filling to create a half-moon shape and seal together the edges. (There are online tutorials for how to crimp the edges like a pro.) Repeat to make 10 dumplings altogether.

04 To cook the dumplings, heat the flavourless oil in a large frying pan over a medium heat. When hot, add the dumplings, flat side down, and fry for 2–3 minutes, until the undersides are golden brown. Add 100ml (3½fl oz) of water to the pan, taking care as the water may spit, then place a lid on the pan. Cook for a further 4–5 minutes, then remove the lid and transfer the dumplings to a serving plate. Leave to cool for a moment or two before serving with the soy dipping sauce.

Thai Basil
Rib of Beef

Serves 2

35 minutes, plus resting

1.7kg (3lb 12oz) beef rib (rump or
    topside would also work well)
generous sprinkling of sea salt
½ teaspoon ground white pepper
2 tablespoons flavourless oil

For the seasoning

2 teaspoons lemongrass paste
2 teaspoons galangal paste
2 teaspoons medium curry powder
2 teaspoons garam masala
2 teaspoons fish sauce
4 teaspoons sweet soy sauce, or light soy
    sauce mixed with 1 tablespoon caster
    (superfine) sugar
4 teaspoons flavourless oil, plus extra to
    season the meat
10 Thai basil leaves, roughly chopped
½ teaspoon ground white pepper
1 red chilli, finely chopped

01 Remove the meat from the fridge 1 hour before you
intend to cook. Season it with the generous sprinkling
of sea salt and the white pepper, and drizzle it on both
sides with the oil. Use your hands to massage in the
seasoning to make sure the meat is well covered, then
set aside.

02 Preheat the oven to 250°C (230°C fan/500°F/Gas 9).

03 Make the seasoning. Mix together all the ingredients
in a bowl – the mixture should be the consistency of
runny honey.

04 Place a large frying pan over a high heat and heat it
almost to smoking point. Place the beef into the pan and
sear it – without moving it – for 8 minutes, until you get
a very delicious, caramelized crust on the underside. Flip
the beef and give it 6 minutes on the other side. Then,
remove it from the heat and transfer it to a baking tray.

05 Pour the seasoning over the meat, making sure to
coat the underside as well. Roast for 15 minutes, until
just medium-rare (if you have a meat thermometer, the
internal temperature should read 45°C/113°F).

06 Remove the beef from the oven and (if you can
wait) leave it to rest for 20 minutes – this way it will
be perfectly medium-rare when you slice into it. ***To
make the Beef, Peanut and Coconut Curry (see page
78), set aside one third of the beef. To make the Crispy
Chilli Beef (see page 77), set aside a further 100g
(3½oz) of the beef. Wrap both portions in foil and
refrigerate for up to 4 days, or thinly slice into strips
and freeze for up to 1 month (defrost before using).***
Slice the remaining beef to serve.

Salt *and* Pepper Potatoes

Serves 2

35 minutes

1kg (2¼lb) new potatoes

2 tablespoons flavourless oil

1 onion, chopped into large dice

1 red (bell) pepper, deseeded and chopped
  into large dice

1 teaspoon dried chilli flakes

½ teaspoon Chinese 5-spice

1 tablespoon runny honey

½ teaspoon salt

½ teaspoon freshly ground black pepper

01 Bring a large saucepan of salted water to a boil over a high heat. Add the potatoes and boil for 15–20 minutes, until they are tender but not too soft. Drain, then set aside.

02 Heat the oil in a large frying pan over a high heat. When hot, add the onion and red (bell) pepper and fry for 2–3 minutes, then sprinkle in the chilli flakes and 5-spice along with the potatoes. Fry for a further 3–4 minutes, then add the honey, salt and pepper. Reduce the heat to low, then finish cooking for 3–4 minutes, until the onion and pepper are tender and the potatoes are coated and glistening. ***To make the Beef, Peanut and Coconut Curry (see page 78), reserve 5 or 6 potatoes in an airtight container. Refrigerate for up to 2 days.***

Pear, Chocolate *and* Cardamom Tart

Serves 6

45 minutes, plus chilling

3 pears peeled, halved and cored

4 tablespoons caster (superfine) sugar

2 star anise

6 cardamom pods, cracked to release
    the seeds

For the base

300g (10oz) Oreo cookies

60g (2oz) unsalted butter, melted

For the ganache

170g (6oz) 70% dark (bittersweet) chocolate

60g (2oz) unsalted butter, cubed

250ml (9fl oz) double (heavy) cream

finely grated zest of 1 orange and juice
    of half

01 Place the pear halves into a medium saucepan with 400ml (14fl oz) of water and the sugar, star anise and seeds of 2 cardamom pods. Cook over a medium heat for 25–30 minutes, until the pears are soft.

02 Meanwhile, make the base. Pulse the Oreos in a food processor until they form a fine crumb. Add the melted butter and pulse again.

03 Tip the Oreo mixture into a 20cm (8in) tart tin. Spread it out and, using your fingertips or the back of a spoon, flatten it over the bottom of the tin and up the sides to create a solid base and crust. Transfer to the fridge for at least 10 minutes to set.

04 Remove the softened pear halves from the poaching syrup with a slotted spoon and use a sharp knife to slice 5 of them lengthways into strips, but leave them attached at the stalk so that you can fan them out. Lay the fanned halves on kitchen paper and pat them dry slightly. Dice the remaining pear half into small pieces. Set aside. ***To make the Pear and Apple Spritz (see page 82), strain the poaching syrup into an airtight container. Refrigerate for up to 2 weeks.***

05 Make the ganache. Put the chocolate and butter into a heatproof bowl. Pour the cream into a small saucepan and add the remaining cardamom seeds. Place the cream mixture over a low heat and warm until just bubbling around the edges. Remove from the heat and pour the mixture through a sieve into the bowl with the chocolate and butter. Leave for 5 minutes to allow the chocolate to melt, then whisk to combine to create a silky, smooth ganache.

06 Remove the Oreo tart shell from the fridge and sprinkle the diced pear in an even layer over the bottom. ***To make the Chocolate Orange Ganache with Seasonal Fruits (see page 80), set aside 100ml (3½fl oz) of the ganache.*** Pour the remaining ganache over the top of the tart and smooth it out. Tap the tin lightly on your work surface to remove any bubbles, then lay the fanned pear halves on top. Refrigerate for 1 hour to set before serving. ***Add the grated orange zest and the juice to the reserved ganache and whisk well. Transfer to an airtight container. Refrigerate for up to 3 days.***

PRAWN TOAST

*If there is an opportunity to eat prawn toast,
I will find it and so it is with the pre-made
dumpling filling in the fridge. Pillowy bread, juicy
prawns and fragrant sesame oil are the perfect
combination of sweet and salty. If you haven't
used sesame oil before, this is a great introduction
to how a little goes a long way (and once you have
some in the cupboard, try a bowl of jasmine rice
with a whisper of sesame oil stirred through –
one of my favourite comfort foods).*

Serves 2   20 minutes

50g (1¾oz) mixed sesame seeds
1 egg white
**6 tablespoons seafood paste from Prawn
    and Scallop Dumplings (see page 68)**
2 spring onions (scallions), thinly sliced (optional)
1 teaspoon sesame oil
3 slices of soft white bread
90ml (3fl oz) flavourless oil, for frying

<u>01</u> Tip the sesame seeds on to a plate and set them
aside for later.

<u>02</u> Tip the egg white into a large mixing bowl and
lightly whisk until frothy, then add in the seafood
paste along with the sliced spring onions (scallions),
if using. Mix well until everything is combined.

<u>03</u> Use a pastry brush to thinly brush a layer of
the sesame oil on to each slice of bread, then spoon
2 tablespoons of the seafood paste mixture on top
and spread it out, so that the bread is completely
covered.

<u>04</u> Place one slice, paste side down, into the
sesame seeds and press lightly so that the seeds
stick. Slice the bread diagonally both ways to make
4 small triangles. Repeat for the other slices.

<u>05</u> To fry, heat a large frying pan over a medium
heat and add the oil. Once hot, place the triangles
of bread into the pan (in batches if necessary),
sesame seed side down. Reduce the heat to
medium-low and fry for 4–5 minutes on each
side, until toasted. Serve straight away.

CRISPY CHILLI BEEF

I am a bit partial to ordering takeaway food when I've had a long day at work – but having beef in the fridge doesn't really give me any reason not to rustle up this easy and delicious remix myself. The cornflour gives the beef strips a super-crunch, and the textured batter soaks up the sweet and spicy sauce. I like to serve this with rice, but you could have it with a salad of grated carrot and cucumber mixed with crunchy shredded lettuce.

Serves 2   20 minutes, plus marinating

100g (3½oz) Thai Basil Rib of Beef (see page 70), thinly sliced into strips
1 egg
1 tablespoon dark soy sauce
1 teaspoon garlic paste
1 teaspoon ginger paste
½ teaspoon sesame oil (optional)
1 teaspoon caster (superfine) sugar
80g (2¾oz) cornflour (corn starch) or rice flour
100ml (3½fl oz) flavourless oil, for frying
50g (1¾oz) unsalted peanuts or cashews
1 teaspoon dried chilli flakes
90ml (3fl oz) runny honey or maple syrup
salt and freshly ground black pepper
1 x 250g pouch of white rice (I like jasmine), reheated, to serve

01 Place the beef strips in a large mixing bowl. Crack the egg into a separate bowl and add the soy sauce, garlic paste, ginger paste, sesame oil (if using) and sugar and beat well with a fork until combined.

02 Pour the mixture over the beef and use a spoon to mix it well to fully coat the beef. Set aside to marinate for 10 minutes.

03 Sprinkle the cornflour (corn starch) or rice flour into a shallow bowl, then carefully turn each strip of beef in it to coat.

04 Heat the oil in a large frying pan over a high heat. When hot, add in the beef strips, in batches if necessary, taking care not to overcrowd the pan. Fry the beef for about 5–6 minutes, turning occasionally, until crispy and golden all over. Set aside each batch on a warmed plate while you cook the remainder, if necessary.

05 Once all the beef is crispy, carefully pour the oil from the pan into a bowl. Add 2 tablespoons of the oil back to the pan, add the nuts, and fry for 1–2 minutes, until coloured, then add back in all the beef. Sprinkle over the chilli flakes and cook for another 1 minute, before drizzling in the honey or maple syrup and tossing the beef to coat. Season generously with salt and pepper and serve with jasmine rice.

BEEF, PEANUT AND COCONUT CURRY

This curry has similar flavour notes to Thailand's massaman curry and feels like a real treat. It's spicy enough to appease those who enjoy a little bit of chilli heat, but tempered with enough sweetness for those who don't. If you have beef left but no potatoes, this still makes a delicious remix recipe; and if you have potatoes but no beef, just add a handful of chopped longstem broccoli in the last 5 minutes to give some bulk.

Serves 2-3   45 minutes

1 teaspoon flavourless oil

⅓ **Thai Basil Rib of Beef (see page 70), thinly sliced into strips**

3 teaspoons red Thai curry paste

1 x 400g can of full-fat coconut milk

1 teaspoon fish sauce

1 teaspoon palm sugar or light brown soft sugar

1 tablespoon peanut butter of choice

5 or 6 Salt and Pepper Potatoes (see page 71) or 150g (5½oz) cooked new potatoes

TO SERVE (OPTIONAL)

1 x 250g pouch of cooked rice (I prefer jasmine), reheated, or 4-6 small flat breads, warmed

a small handful of coriander (cilantro), leaves picked and chopped

1 tablespoon unsalted roasted peanuts, chopped

1 red chilli, deseeded and chopped

01 Heat the oil in a large frying pan over a medium heat. When hot, add the beef and curry paste and allow them to cook for 1-2 minutes. Then, add the coconut milk, fish sauce and sugar and reduce the heat to a low simmer.

02 Cook at a simmer for 25 minutes, then add the peanut butter and potatoes and simmer for a further 10 minutes, until all the flavours are melded and everything is heated through.

03 Serve with cooked rice or warmed flat breads, and sprinkled with coriander (cilantro), peanuts and chilli, if you like.

CHOCOLATE ORANGE GANACHE WITH SEASONAL FRUITS

Do you know the best time of the week to have a chocolate fondue? It's anytime you have a pot of leftover ganache in the fridge. If you have friends visiting, this is such a fun addition to the table served with any fresh fruits you have in the house. Equally, though, time spent working from home can be exponentially improved with a spoonful of warmed ganache and a handful of strawberries.

Serves 2   10 minutes

100ml (3½fl oz) chocolate orange ganache
    from Pear, Chocolate and Cardamom Tart
    (see page 74)
3 tablespoons single (light) cream, to loosen
    (optional)
seasonal fruits, cut into bitesize pieces

01 Place the chocolate orange ganache in a small saucepan over a low heat. Add the single (light) cream, to loosen it, if you like, and stir as the ganache melts and becomes more liquid again. Keep heating until it is properly warmed through. (You can do this in the microwave, if you prefer – on medium power in 10-second bursts.)

02 Transfer the warmed ganache into a serving bowl and serve straight away with the fruit pieces for dipping.

PEAR AND
APPLE SPRITZ

Turning leftover fruit syrups into delicious drinks feels like the absolute height of thrifty sophistication to me. Pear and apple go gorgeously with the bright, spirited flavour of star anise and make the perfect autumn spritz. I like to make this with sparkling water and lots of ice, but it would be equally good with sparkling white wine.

Serves 2   10 minutes, plus cooling

**130ml (4½fl oz) poaching syrup from
Pear, Chocolate and Cardamom Tart
(see page 74)**
2 teaspoons caster (superfine) sugar
ice cubes
150ml (5fl oz) cloudy apple juice
about 50ml (1¾fl oz) sparkling water
2 rosemary sprigs, to serve (optional)

01 Pour the poaching syrup into a small saucepan, add the sugar and place the pan over a medium heat. Bring to a gentle boil and allow to bubble and reduce for about 5 minutes, until thick and syrupy and reduced by about half. Leave to cool completely.

02 Once the syrup is cool, fill 2 tall glasses with ice cubes. Add 2 tablespoons of syrup to each glass along with equal amounts of the apple juice. Top up with the sparkling water and stir. If you like, finish off each glass with a sprig of rosemary for a gorgeous autumnal mocktail!

Cheddar *and* Chive Flat Breads *with* Roasted Tomatoes

Serves 4

35 minutes

50g (1¾oz) mature cheddar, grated

a small bunch of chives, chopped,
    plus extra to serve

250ml (9fl oz) double (heavy) cream

1kg (2¼lb) cherry tomatoes

2 tablespoons flavourless oil

1 garlic bulb, cloves separated and
    finely sliced

1 teaspoon freshly ground black pepper

2 red chillies, deseeded and finely chopped

2 tablespoons red wine vinegar (or sherry
    or white wine vinegar)

1 tablespoon runny honey or light brown
    soft sugar

4 small flat breads

01 Preheat the oven to 220°C (200°C fan/425°F/Gas 7).

02 Place the cheddar in a mixing bowl, then add the chopped chives and pour over the cream. Use a hand-held electric blender to blitz everything together – the mixture should be thick but not overly stiff. ***To make the Cheddar and Chive Toasties (see page 92), reserve 6 tablespoons of the mixture in an airtight container. Refrigerate for up to 5 days.*** Set the remaining mixture aside.

03 Place the tomatoes in a baking tray with the oil, garlic, pepper and chillies. Bake for 20 minutes, until the tomatoes begin to burst, then remove them from the oven and gently squash them a little with a spoon. Sprinkle over the vinegar and honey or sugar, and return to the oven for 5 minutes, until the liquid has reduced to a sticky glaze. ***To make the Simple Tomato Pasta (see page 93), reserve 20 of the tomatoes and some of the juice in an airtight container. Refrigerate for up to 4 days.*** Set the tomatoes aside, but leave the oven on.

04 Place the flat breads on a separate baking tray. Pop a spoonful of the cheddar cream on top of each and spread it out evenly using a knife. Place the flat breads into the oven for 5 minutes to warm through, then finish with a scattering of the remaining tomatoes and an extra sprinkling of chives.

Honey *and* Bay Roasted Ham

Serves 4

2 hours 20 minutes

1.2kg (2lb 10oz) cured, smoked ham or
   gammon joint
2 leeks, sliced into 2cm (¾in) rounds
4 bay leaves
1 tablespoon freshly ground black pepper
3 tablespoons mustard powder
90ml (3fl oz) runny honey

01 Preheat the oven to 210°C (190°C fan/415°F/Gas 6–7).

02 Using a sharp knife, score diagonal cuts into the skin of the ham or gammon joint, taking care not to cut into the flesh.

03 Place the leeks in a layer in a baking dish and place the ham on top. Scatter the bay leaves and pepper around the joint.

04 Measure out 600ml (1 pint) of water into a jug and stir in the mustard powder and 2 tablespoons of the honey, then pour the mixture around the ham, making sure the meat isn't completely covered as you want the top to get crispy.

05 Place a lid on the baking dish or cover it tightly with foil (don't leave any gaps – you don't want the steam to escape), and roast it in the centre of the oven for 2 hours, or until the ham is cooked through. Remove the lid or foil, drizzle the remaining honey over the ham and return the baking dish, uncovered, to the oven for 10 minutes for the ham to glaze.

06 Remove the ham and the bay leaves from the liquid using tongs. Discard the bay leaves. ***To make the Ham Stock Potatoes (see page 95), pour the leftover ham stock, including the leeks, into an airtight container. Refrigerate for up to 4 days, or freeze for up to 1 month (defrost before using). To make the Hawaiian Fried Rice (see page 96), slice off one third of the ham (150g/5½oz). Leave it to cool, then cut it into 2cm (¾in) dice and transfer to an airtight container. Refrigerate for up to 4 days, or freeze for up to 1 month (it will cook from frozen). To make the Jambon Beurre (see page 94), slice off 4 thick slices from the remaining joint and place in an airtight container. Refrigerate or freeze as for the diced ham (but defrost before using).*** Keep the remaining ham warm until you're ready to serve.

Roasted Garlic *and* Rosemary Swede Wedges

Serves 4

55 minutes

4 tablespoons flavourless oil

1 large swede, peeled and cut into 8 wedges

3 rosemary sprigs, leaves picked

1 garlic bulb

1 teaspoon runny honey (optional)

¼ teaspoon ground white pepper

¼ teaspoon sea salt

01 Preheat the oven to 240°C (220°C fan/475°F/Gas 8).

02 Drizzle the oil into a baking tray and add the swede, turning the wedges to coat them in the oil. Scatter the rosemary leaves over the top.

03 Wrap the garlic bulb in foil to completely enclose and place this into the tray with the swede. Bake in the centre of the oven for 40 minutes, until the swede is tender. Remove from the oven.

04 When the garlic is cool enough to handle, unwrap it, then slice the bulb in half through its middle. Squeeze out the garlic flesh from one half over the swede (use a spoon to help you). Set aside the other half (see tip, below). Return the swede to the oven and bake for a further 5 minutes, to caramelize. Remove from the oven. To finish, drizzle over the honey (if using) and sprinkle over the white pepper and sea salt. ***To make the Roasted Swede and Miso Puy Lentils (see page 98), set aside 2 of the wedges and leave to cool. Wrap them in cling film, then refrigerate for up to 2 days.***

Chef's tip: Pour 150ml (5fl oz) flavourless oil into a sealable jar. Add the remaining roasted half garlic bulb and shake well. Set aside for at least 1 week, then use the oil to add flavour to breads, pastas and salad dressings.

Orange Cakes
with Earl Grey Custard

Makes 12

35 minutes

170g (6oz) unsalted butter, very softened,
   plus extra for greasing
190g (6½oz/1¼ cups) plain (all-purpose)
   flour
1 teaspoon bicarbonate of soda (baking
   soda)
finely grated zest of 3 oranges, plus 100ml
   (3½fl oz) juice (slice the remaining
   orange flesh, to serve)
120g (4¼oz/½ cup + 2 teaspoons) caster
   (superfine) sugar
4 eggs
1 teaspoon vanilla paste

For the custard

200ml (7fl oz) whole milk
150ml (5fl oz) double (heavy) cream
2 teaspoons Earl Grey tea leaves or
   3 Earl Grey tea bags
3 egg yolks
40g (1¼oz/2 tablespoons + 2 teaspoons)
   caster (superfine) sugar
1 teaspoon cornflour (corn starch)
1 teaspoon vanilla paste

01 Preheat the oven to 210°C (190°C fan/415°F/Gas 6–7). Grease a 12-cup muffin tray with a little butter.

02 Put the flour, bicarbonate of soda (baking soda), orange zest and caster (superfine) sugar in a large mixing bowl and stir to combine.

03 Put the softened butter in a separate bowl, then crack in the eggs. Add the orange juice and vanilla and use a balloon whisk or an electric hand mixer to beat them together for 3 minutes, until fully combined and fluffy.

04 Tip the butter and egg mixture into the dry ingredients and beat with the whisk or mixer until no flour streaks remain. The mixture should be combined, thick and smooth.

05 Spoon 3 tablespoons of the mixture into each of the cups in the muffin tray. Bake in the centre of the oven for 15 minutes, until the cakes are risen and golden and a skewer inserted into the centres comes out clean. Set aside the cakes, in the tray, to cool.

06 Meanwhile, make the custard. Pour the milk and cream into a medium saucepan. Add the tea leaves or tea bags and bring the liquid to a gentle simmer.

07 Tip the egg yolks into a bowl and add the caster sugar, cornflour (corn starch) and vanilla and whisk until the mixture is pale and creamy. Once the milk is hot, strain it into a heatproof jug to remove the tea if necessary (or remove the tea bags), then pour it into the bowl with the egg-yolk mixture, whisking all the time to create a loose custard.

08 Tip the custard back into the pan over a low–medium heat. Stir for 6–8 minutes, until the mixture begins to thicken, then turn off the heat. If you like, strain the custard to make sure it's completely smooth. To serve, plate up 1 cake per person, add a couple of orange slices, and pour over some of the custard. ***To make the Tea-and-Biscuit Pots (see page 99), pour individual portions of the remaining custard into pots or ramekins. Cover and refrigerate for up to 4 days.***

CHEDDAR AND CHIVE TOASTIES

Toasties are an elite food group and I won't hear otherwise. They take the beauty of the sandwich and say "Yes, this – but also melty and delicious." Because you're using the cheese-and-chive cream from page 83 for this remix, it's super-melty and light. If you like, you could add a spoonful of your favourite chutney or a slice of your favourite sandwich meat, too.

Serves 2   10 minutes, plus resting

4 slices of soft white bread
6 tablespoons cheese-and-chive cream from Cheddar and Chive Flat Breads with Roasted Tomatoes (see page 83)
1 large tomato, cut into 8 slices
1 tablespoon unsalted butter

01 Place 2 slices of the bread on your work top. Spread half the cheese-and-chive cream over each slice and top each with 4 slices of tomato. Place a second slice of bread on top of each to sandwich.

02 Melt the butter in a large frying pan over a medium heat. Place both sandwiches into the pan and cook for 3–4 minutes on each side, until the bread is golden and toasted all over.

03 Remove the toasties from the pan and allow them to rest for 2 minutes before tucking in.

SIMPLE TOMATO PASTA

This pasta has no airs and graces, but what it lacks in sophistication, it makes up for in flavours and nourishment. Parmesan really boosts the flavour of the tomatoes, using something called synergistic umami, which all sounds very scientific but simply means that tomatoes and cheese are, and always should be, the very best of friends.

Serves 2   15 minutes

200g (7oz) dried pasta of choice
20 roasted tomatoes from Cheddar and Chive Flat Breads with Roasted Tomatoes (see page 83)
30g (1oz) parmesan, grated
salt

01 Bring a large saucepan of salted water to a boil. Add the pasta and cook according to the packet instructions, until al dente.

02 Meanwhile, heat the tomatoes in a frying pan over a medium heat. Add the parmesan and a cupful of the pasta cooking water. Allow the sauce to bubble and thicken and become silky (about 2-3 minutes).

03 Drain the cooked pasta and tip it into the pan with the tomato sauce. Warm through together for 1 minute, stirring to coat the pasta in the sauce. Serve straight away.

JAMBON BEURRE

Otherwise known as ham, butter and pickle baguette, this is my most trusted sandwich. I'll happily pick one up at a café when I'm out and about, but making it at home with home-baked ham creates a thing of true beauty. If you don't have cornichons or bread-and-butter pickles, you could use any other pickles you like.

Serves 2   5 minutes

2 small baguettes
about 3 tablespoons salted butter
6 small cornichons or halved bread-and-butter
    pickles
**4 thick slices of Honey and Bay Roasted Ham
    (see page 86)**

01 Slice the baguettes in half along their length. Butter the cut sides and fill the baguettes with equal amounts of cornichons or pickles and ham. Enjoy!

HAM STOCK POTATOES

If you're a fan of dauphinoise potatoes, then you're going to love these. There's something very homely about saving the cooking stock from the ham to make this remix – a real sense of using everything up and nothing going to waste. If you've frozen the stock, let it defrost first.

Serves 2   50 minutes

1 tablespoon flavourless oil, for greasing
400ml (14fl oz) chilled stock from Honey and Bay Roasted Ham (see page 86)
3 large potatoes, peeled and thinly sliced
60g (2oz) mature cheddar, grated
100ml (3½fl oz) boiling water from a kettle

01 Preheat the oven to 220°C (200°C fan/425°F/ Gas 7). Grease a 20cm (8in) round baking dish with the oil.

02 Using a spoon, gently remove the first layer of fat from the ham stock and discard (using chilled stock will make it easier to remove this layer).

03 Lay the first layer of potatoes into the baking dish, making sure to completely cover the base, then spoon over 1 generous tablespoon of the ham stock, using the back of the spoon to spread it over the potatoes. If there are any leeks in the ham stock, gently break them up. Sprinkle over a little cheese.

04 Continue to layer the potatoes, stock and cheese until you run out of potatoes, finishing with a layer of stock and making sure you have enough cheese in reserve to sprinkle over the top in the next step.

05 Finally, mix the remaining ham stock with the boiling water and pour it over the contents of the dish. Scatter over the remaining cheese and then place the dish in the centre of the oven to bake for 35–40 minutes, until tender. Serve straight away.

HAWAIIAN FRIED RICE

This rice is one of my go-to weekly meals. The soy sauce holds everything together, but other than that feel free to play around with the ingredients, using up whatever you have in the fridge. Leafy greens make a great stand-in for peas, onion for spring onion, tomatoes for red peppers. You could even use prawns in place of the ham, if you're not remixing from page 86. Using a pouch of ready-cooked rice makes it super-easy to put together.

Serves 4   15 minutes

2 eggs
4 tablespoons garlic paste
4 tablespoons ginger paste
4 tablespoons light soy sauce
1 tablespoon Maggi's liquid seasoning (or other umami-rich liquid seasoning; optional but recommended)
2 teaspoons sesame oil
1 tablespoon caster (superfine) sugar or runny honey
3 tablespoons flavourless oil
1 red (bell) pepper, deseeded and diced
1 yellow (bell) pepper, deseeded and diced
100g (3½oz) fresh or frozen peas
100g (3½oz) cubed pineapple (fresh or drained canned)
3 spring onions (scallions), thinly sliced, plus extra to serve if you like
150g (5½oz) diced Honey and Bay Roasted Ham (see page 86)
1 x 250g pouch of cooked rice (I prefer jasmine)

01 Crack the eggs into a small bowl and add half each of the garlic paste, ginger paste, soy sauce and liquid seasoning and beat with a fork to break up the eggs. Set aside.

02 In a separate small bowl, mix the remaining soy sauce with the sesame oil, caster (superfine) sugar or honey and remaining liquid seasoning along with 120ml (4fl oz) of water.

03 Place a large frying pan or a wok over a high heat and pour in the flavourless oil. Add the (bell) peppers, peas, pineapple and the spring onions (scallions) along with the remaining garlic and ginger pastes and fry for 3–4 minutes, using a spoon to move the ingredients around so that they don't stick.

04 Push the contents of the pan to one side and pour the egg mixture into the space. Use the spoon to gently move the eggs around until they begin to scramble, then combine everything in the pan together.

05 Add the ham and cook, stirring, for 2 minutes, then add the cooked rice, using a wooden spoon to break it up and mix it in. Pour in the soy sauce and sugar mixture, mixing well, and stir-fry for a further 2–3 minutes, until everything is piping hot throughout. Serve with extra spring onions sprinkled on top, if you like.

ROASTED SWEDE AND MISO PUY LENTILS

When I was growing up, swede used to be a vegetable reserved for making mash, which is still one of my favourite ways to eat it. However, roasted swede really is something special. The edges go almost fudge-like and sweet without losing the distinctive earthy flavour. If you don't have any miso, this remix will still be delicious, but if you can get your hands on some, you won't regret it.

Serves 2   20 minutes

1 onion, halved and thinly sliced
1 tablespoon flavourless oil
1 teaspoon unsalted butter
1 teaspoon white miso (optional)
2 Roasted Garlic and Rosemary Swede Wedges (see page 89), diced into small pieces
1 x 250g pouch of cooked puy lentils
30g (1oz) parmesan or other strong cheese, grated (optional)
salt

01 Place the onion into a medium saucepan with a lid. Season with a little salt, add the oil and mix well. Place the lid on the pan and place the pan over a low heat. Leave to sweat for 10 minutes, until softened.

02 Remove the lid and add the butter and the miso (if using), stirring well with a wooden spoon to make a sauce. Cook for a further 2 minutes, then add the swede and lentils, breaking up the lentils with a spoon.

03 Add about 3 tablespoons of water and stir to combine, then cook over a low heat for 5 minutes, until piping hot. Serve in bowls, sprinkled with cheese, if you wish.

TEA-AND-BISCUIT POTS

I know that this is barely a recipe, but equally it feels like the most British recipe I've ever written and it's perfect for a working day when you need a sweet treat – and I don't even mean at the end of the day. If you need a pick-me-up at lunchtime, have the custard in a little airtight pot with you and crumble in your biscuits on the go. Your co-workers with their yogurt pots will look on in envy. Feel free to substitute the custard creams for any of your favourite biscuits, if you prefer.

Serves according to leftover custard   5 minutes

2 custard cream biscuits per pot
individual chilled pots of leftover Earl Grey custard from Orange Cakes with Earl Grey Custard (see page 90)

01 Place the custard creams into a food bag and use a rolling pin to smash them up into small pieces. Sprinkle them equally over the custard pots and enjoy for the easiest mid-week dessert.

Samosa Chaat

Makes 12

1 hour, plus resting

For the dough

300g (10oz) plain (all-purpose) flour

1 teaspoon nigella seeds

1 teaspoon ajwain seeds (optional)

a large pinch of salt, plus extra to season

4 tablespoons flavourless oil, plus 500ml
(16fl oz) for deep frying

For the filling

4 long red chillies

3 long green chillies

10 garlic cloves

2 tablespoons ginger paste

2 shallots

4 tablespoons flavourless oil

1 x 400g can of chickpeas (garbanzos),
drained and rinsed

1 teaspoon medium curry powder

1 heaped tablespoon garam masala

1 tablespoon ground coriander

3 tablespoons tomato ketchup

1 x 400g can of chopped tomatoes

For the green chutney

a large handful of mint, leaves picked and
roughly chopped

a large handful of coriander (cilantro),
leaves and stalks roughly chopped

1 teaspoon garam masala

1 teaspoon caster (superfine) sugar

90g (3oz) full-fat plain yogurt, plus extra
if needed

For the toppings (optional)

full-fat plain yogurt, tamarind chutney, sev,
pomegranate seeds, coriander (cilantro) leaves

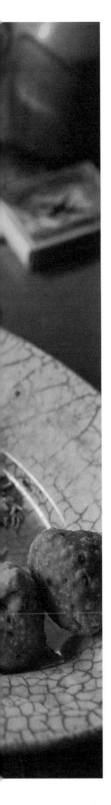

01 For the dough, tip the flour into a large mixing bowl and add the nigella seeds, the ajwain seeds (if using), and the salt. Pour in the oil and use your fingers to rub the oil into the flour for a few minutes to create a breadcrumb-like texture.

02 Once the mixture easily forms a ball in your hand when pressed together, add water, a little at a time (up to about 1 tablespoon altogether), to create a firm dough. Take care not to overwork it – you want to bring it together into a firm ball (it will soften up once it has been rested). Cover with a damp cloth and leave to rest for 45 minutes.

03 Meanwhile, make the filling. Place the chillies, garlic, ginger paste, shallots and oil in a food processor with a generous seasoning of salt and pulse to make a paste.

04 Heat a frying pan over a low heat and spoon or pour in the paste. Place a lid on the pan and cook for 15 minutes, taking the lid off every 5 minutes to give everything a stir, until the paste is softened and aromatic. If the mixture becomes dry and begins to stick to the pan, add a splash of water.

05 Remove the lid and add the chickpeas (garbanzos), curry powder, garam masala and ground coriander. Cook for 2–3 minutes to toast the spices. Add the ketchup and tomatoes, stir well and simmer for 10–15 minutes, until the chickpeas are tender. Turn off the heat and leave to cool. *To make the Loaded Chickpea Pachos (see page 108), spoon 100g (3½oz) of the chickpea mixture into an airtight container. Refrigerate for up to 3 days.*

06 While the filling is cooling, make the chutney. Place all the chutney ingredients into a clean food processor and blitz until completely smooth. If the mixture is too thick, add a little more yogurt and blitz again to combine. Set aside.

07 Once the dough has rested, divide it into 12 equal portions. Make the samosas one by one, keeping the other portions of dough covered with a damp tea towel while you work. One at a time, shape each portion into a ball, then, using a rolling pin, roll it into a 10cm (4in) disc and cut it in half to create 2 semicircles.

08 Take a semicircle of dough into the palm of your hand and bring the two curved edges together, pressing them gently to create a cone. Add 1 tablespoon of the cooked chickpea mixture into the middle of the cone, then press together the open edge, encasing the filling. Set aside on a plate lined with greaseproof paper while you fill the other semicircle. Shape, roll, cut and fill the remaining dough portions in the same way to give 12 samosas altogether (you'll have filling left over).

09 To cook, pour the 500ml (16fl oz) flavourless oil into a deep, heavy-based saucepan and heat it to 180°C (350°F) on a cooking thermometer. Or, drop a 1cm (½in) cube of day-old bread into the oil – the oil is hot enough if the bread sizzles, rises to the surface and turns golden within 1 minute. (Alternatively, use a deep-fat fryer.)

10 Three or four at a time, deep-fry the samosas for 3–4 minutes, using a slotted spoon to turn them, until they are golden brown all over. Remove from the oil and set aside to drain on kitchen paper. Allow the oil to come back up to frying temperature before cooking the next batch.

11 To serve, add a layer of yogurt (if using), tablespoons of the remaining chickpea mixture (warmed if you wish) and drizzles of tamarind chutney (if using) to a serving dish. Top with the samosas, drizzle with some green chutney and sprinkle with sev, pomegranate seeds, tamarind chutney and extra coriander, if you like (you'll need the rest of the green chutney to serve with the menu recipe on page 104).

Paneer, Green Lentil *and* Cashew Curry

Serves 4

50 minutes

4 tablespoons flavourless oil

2 onions, halved and sliced

1 x 500g pouch of diced paneer

8 garlic cloves, finely chopped

1 long red chilli, finely chopped

1 long green chilli, finely chopped

2.5cm (1in) piece of fresh ginger, peeled
and finely chopped

250g (9oz) dried green lentils, rinsed in
cold water

500ml (16fl oz) boiling water from a kettle

100g (3½oz) cashews

50g (1¾oz) desiccated (shredded) coconut

salt (optional)

For the spice mix

1 teaspoon ground coriander

1 teaspoon ground cinnamon

½ teaspoon ground turmeric

1 teaspoon sweet smoked paprika

1 teaspoon medium curry powder

To serve

1 x 250g pouch of cooked basmati rice,
reheated, or 4 small flat breads,
or roti, warmed

a small handful of mint leaves, torn

01 Preheat the oven to 220°C (200°C fan/425°F/Gas 7). Combine all of the spices for the spice mix in a small bowl and set aside.

02 Heat half the oil in a large saucepan over a medium heat. When hot, add the onions and cook for 3–4 minutes, until slightly softened, then add the paneer, garlic, both chillies, and the ginger and cook for a further 8–10 minutes, until the paneer has browned slightly. *To make the Spicy and Sweet Paneer (see page 110), transfer 250g (9oz) of the paneer mixture to an airtight container. Refrigerate for up to 3 days.* Scoop out the remaining mixture from the pan and set aside.

03 Add the remaining oil along with the spice mix to the pan and cook for 1 minute over a medium heat, until the spices are toasted and aromatic. Add the lentils and boiling water and give everything a stir to make sure that nothing is stuck to the bottom of the pan. Simmer for 20 minutes, until the lentils are starting to soften.

04 Meanwhile, tip the cashews on to one half of a baking tray and scatter the coconut on to the other half. Bake for 8–10 minutes, until both are deeply golden.

05 Add the paneer mixture to the pan with the lentils, along with half the toasted cashews and all the toasted coconut. Simmer over a low heat for 10 minutes, until the lentils are fully soft. If you need to season with salt, add it only once the lentils are cooked (otherwise the salt stops the lentils from softening).

06 Serve the curry with rice, flat breads or roti, and scattered with the remaining cashews and some torn mint leaves. *To make the Mushroom and Lentil Sausage Casserole (see page 109), spoon any leftover curry into an airtight container. Refrigerate for up to 3 days.*

Sweet Potatoes *with* Mustard, Pomegranate, Chutneys *and* Puffed Rice

Serves 4

55 minutes, plus cooling

flavourless oil, for oiling the tray

6 sweet potatoes (I like to use purple and
   orange for colour)

50g (1¾oz) puffed rice

1 teaspoon medium curry powder

2 tablespoons wholegrain mustard

¼ teaspoon cayenne pepper (optional)

1 tablespoon full-fat plain yogurt

leftover Green Chutney (see page 100),
   to taste

50g (1¾oz) pomegranate seeds

a couple of coriander (cilantro) sprigs

salt and freshly ground black pepper

01 Preheat the oven to 220°C (200°C fan/425°F/Gas 7).

02 Lightly oil a large baking tray. Place the sweet potatoes into the tray and bake in the centre of the oven for 30–45 minutes, until the insides are soft and the skins are coming away from the flesh. ***To make the Sweet Potato Katsu (see page 113), set aside 2 potatoes, leave them to cool, then place them in an airtight container. Refrigerate for up to 3 days.***

03 Tip the puffed rice into a small mixing bowl and sprinkle over the curry powder. Toss to coat.

04 Meanwhile, leave the baked sweet potatoes to cool for 10 minutes, then slice them lengthways in half. Scoop all the flesh into a large mixing bowl, reserving the potato skins. Add the mustard and the cayenne pepper (if using) and season well with salt and pepper. Mash with a fork to combine. Place the skins on a serving platter, then spoon the flavoured mash back into them.

05 Stir the yogurt well so that it's slightly runny and drizzle it over the top of the loaded sweet potatoes. Drizzle the chutney over, and then top with the pomegranate seeds, coriander (cilantro) sprigs and puffed rice.

Gulab Jamun
with Kiwi Fruit

Serves 4

20 minutes, plus soaking

70g (2¼oz) milk powder

3 tablespoons plain (all-purpose) flour

½ teaspoon baking powder

30g (1oz) unsalted butter, melted

50ml (1¾fl oz) whole milk

500ml (16fl oz) flavourless oil, for
    deep frying

For the syrup

200g (7oz/1 cup) demerara sugar

6 cardamom pods, cracked

2 cinnamon sticks

1 star anise

1 teaspoon vanilla paste

To serve

300ml (10fl oz) double (heavy) cream

2 kiwis, peeled and each cut into 4 slices

01 Mix together the milk powder, flour and baking powder in a large mixing bowl. Pour in the melted butter and use your hands to mix everything together to a breadcrumb-like texture. Make a well in the centre and add the milk, then bring the mixture together using your hands until you have a soft ball of dough. Cover and leave to rest for 10 minutes while you make the sugar syrup.

02 Place all the syrup ingredients in a medium saucepan with 200ml (7fl oz) of water over a medium heat. Bring the liquid to a boil, then boil for 2 minutes, until the sugar has dissolved and the syrup is thick. Turn off the heat and strain the syrup through a sieve into a serving dish. ***To make the Chai Latte (see page 113), place the used cinnamon sticks and cardamom pods into a sterilized jam jar. Ladle in roughly one third of the syrup. Seal and refrigerate for up to 1 week.***

03 Break up the dough into 8 equal pieces and roll each piece into a golf-ball-sized ball.

04 Pour the oil into a deep, heavy-based saucepan and heat it to 150°C (300°F) on a cooking thermometer, or until a cube of day-old bread sizzles and turns golden within 2 minutes. (Alternatively, use a deep-fat fryer.) Place 4 of the jamun balls into the hot oil and use a slotted spoon to move them around for 3–4 minutes, until cooked through and golden.

05 Scoop out the cooked balls and place them into the serving dish with the syrup. Repeat with the remaining balls. Leave the balls to soak in the syrup for at least 1 hour (or up to a week in the fridge) before serving.

06 To serve, whip the cream to soft peaks. Make a slit in the middle of each gulab jamun, spoon in some cream and finish with a slice of kiwi fruit.

LOADED CHICKPEA PACHOS

Pachos – poppadom nachos, get it?! These are delicious and every movie night needs them. You will be shocked at what reserving a couple or so tablespoons of chickpeas can yield! Feel free to substitute the mozzarella for any cheese you have in the fridge and pile on top anything else you fancy. Enjoy!

Serves 2   20 minutes

70g (2¼oz) bag of mini poppadoms
    (or use tortilla chips)
60g (2oz) cooking mozzarella, grated
    (or use any cheese you have), plus extra
    for the topping
**100g (3½oz) chickpea filling from Samosa Chaat
(see page 100)**

FOR THE TOPPINGS
4 tablespoons tamarind chutney
90ml (3fl oz) full-fat plain yogurt
1 tablespoon mint sauce
a small handful of pomegranate seeds
a small handful of coriander (cilantro) leaves

01 Preheat the oven to 200°C (180°C fan/400°F/ Gas 6).

02 Place the poppadoms into a baking dish with the grated cheese and mix everything together to make sure the cheese is evenly distributed.

03 Spoon the chickpea filling all over the poppadoms and sprinkle some extra cheese on top. Bake the pachos for 15 minutes, until warmed through and the cheese has melted.

04 Remove from the oven and sprinkle over all of the toppings. Serve straight away.

MUSHROOM AND LENTIL SAUSAGE CASSEROLE

This recipe uses the remainder of the packet of dried lentils you had from the Paneer, Green Lentil and Cashew Curry. Plus, if you have any of the curry itself left, you can use that in the base as well, making this the perfect no-waste midweek supper.

Serves 2   40 minutes

1 onion, sliced into rounds
3 tablespoons flavourless oil
250g (9oz) dried green lentils, rinsed in cold water
500ml (16fl oz) boiling water from a kettle
4 chestnut mushrooms, quartered (optional)
4 meat or meat-free sausages
1 tablespoon brown miso
1 tablespoon unsalted butter
leftover Paneer, Green Lentil and Cashew Curry (see page 102), if available
salt and freshly ground black pepper
a small handful of chives, finely chopped, to serve (optional)
30g (1oz) mature cheddar, grated, to serve (optional)

01 Preheat the oven to 220°C (200°C fan/ 425°F/Gas 7).

02 Place the onion in a medium saucepan and drizzle with 2 tablespoons of the oil, then stir well. Place the pan over a medium heat and cook the onion for 5 minutes, until translucent. (Don't season the onions at this point, as the salt will stop the lentils from cooking in the next step.)

03 Add the lentils and boiling water and stir well. Simmer for 20 minutes, or until the lentils are soft.

04 Meanwhile, place the mushrooms and sausages into a baking tray and coat them in the remaining oil. Season with salt and pepper, then bake for 15–20 minutes, until the sausages are golden and cooked through.

05 Add the miso, butter and a generous seasoning of salt and pepper to the cooked lentils, along with the leftover curry if you have it, and tip in the sausages and mushrooms. Cover the pan and cook the casserole for a further 10 minutes, allowing the lentils to go from soft to truly silky.

06 Serve in wide bowls, sprinkled with chives and cheese, if you like.

SPICY AND SWEET PANEER

There is a Sri Lankan restaurant near my house that makes the most amazing paneer I've ever tasted in my life, and also the spiciest. I've done my best to make a version of it in this remix - keeping it a little easier on the heat. This is delicious both hot and cold, served with rice, or just as it is.

Serves 2   15 minutes

2 tablespoons flavourless oil
3 garlic cloves, thinly sliced
30g (1oz) cashews
1 orange or red (bell) pepper, deseeded and sliced
    into strips
1 onion, sliced
250g (9oz) diced paneer mixture from Paneer,
    Green Lentil and Cashew Curry (see page
    102)
6 cherry tomatoes, halved
1 teaspoon dried chilli flakes
1 tablespoon palm sugar or caster (superfine)
    sugar
salt and freshly ground black pepper
1 x 250g pouch of cooked rice of your choice,
    reheated, to serve (optional)

01 Heat the oil in a large frying pan over a high heat. When hot, add the garlic and cashews and fry for 1 minute. Then, add the (bell) pepper and onion and cook for 3-4 minutes, until softened. Add the paneer mixture and cook for a further 3-4 minutes to warm through. Tip in the tomatoes, chilli flakes and sugar and stir to combine. Cook for 1 minute more, then add about 3 tablespoons of water.

02 Cook, still over a high heat, for about 3-4 minutes, until the sauce is bubbling and thickened. Season with salt and pepper and serve with cooked rice, or just as it is.

SWEET POTATO KATSU

Serves 2   30 minutes

2 baked sweet potatoes from Sweet Potatoes
    with Mustard, Pomegranate, Chutneys
    and Puffed Rice (see page 104)
70g (2¼oz) panko breadcrumbs
100g (3½oz) plain (all-purpose) flour
1 egg
3 tablespoons whole milk or water
flavourless oil, for spritzing
salt and ground white pepper
1 x 250g pouch of cooked rice, reheated, to serve
2 cubes of a katsu sauce block dissolved in
    400ml (14fl oz) boiling water, to serve

01 Preheat the oven to 230°C (210°C fan/450°F/
Gas 8). Line up two plates on your work surface and
one bowl. Line a baking tray with greaseproof paper.

02 Remove the skins from the sweet potatoes and
place the flesh into a mixing bowl. Season with salt
and white pepper and use your hands to combine.

03 Tip the breadcrumbs on to one of the plates and
the flour on to the other; crack the egg into the bowl.
Add the milk or water to the egg and combine.

04 Divide the sweet potato into 4 equal portions,
flattening each out in the palm of your hand to about
3cm (1¼in) thick. Gently place the potato patty into
the flour, then turn it to coat both sides. Very gently
place the patty into the egg mixture, submerging it
fully, then straight into the breadcrumbs, evenly
coating each side to make a sweet-potato katsu.

05 Place the katsu on the baking tray and repeat the
process until you have 4 altogether. Spritz the katsu
with oil and bake for 20 minutes, until browned.
Serve with cooked white rice, and with Japanese
curry (katsu) sauce for dipping.

CHAI LATTE

Serves 1   5 minutes

150ml (5fl oz) whole milk
1 tablespoon syrup from Gulab Jamun
    with Kiwi Fruit (see page 107)
1 shot of espresso coffee
small piece of fresh ginger, peeled and grated
    (to give about ½ teaspoon; optional)

01 Pour the milk into a small saucepan over
a low-medium heat. Add the syrup and bring
the liquid to a boil.

02 Meanwhile, pour the espresso shot into
a coffee mug.

03 Once the milk mixture is boiling, add the
grated ginger (if using) and simmer for 1 minute
to infuse.

04 Pour the infused hot milk over the espresso
and enjoy (there's no need to strain it).

Winter

Winter in Newcastle, where I'm from, is a time of great tradition – it's also freezing cold! This chapter is filled with jovial and fun dishes to share with family and friends when hunkering down and keeping warm are the order of the day, and when you especially need to keep your heart and belly full.

My appetite for something baked or roasted, and for pastry (sweet or savoury; rolled, shaped or crumbled) is never more awake than when it's cold outside. Warming soups, bean stews, rich sauces and spicy jams, too. All these, and more, make an appearance in the menus and remixes in this chapter.

The first winter menu – which I've called **This green and pleasant land** – is a vegetarian feast that ticks all my boxes. It starts out by making the most of winter's best banana shallots, turning them into something sticky, sweet and comforting to serve with crunchy pakoras. The main – a veggie pie that is all the best of the veg in a traditional roast, plus the stuffing, wrapped in puff pastry and served with a sophisticated, herby twist on cauliflower cheese – is pastry and sauce right there (and not a word from the non-veggies: I guarantee you won't miss the meat). And for dessert – crumble, naturally. Winter isn't an obvious season for rhubarb, but it works so beautifully with the best of the winter oranges that I couldn't resist – this crumble is a sensory explosion on your tongue.

I've brought spice to menu eight – **The temper of saccharine** – because it warms from within. Spicy sausage and chilli oil feature in the starter, and a main of whole roasted duck is absolutely a recipe to be shared among friends in warm conviviality. I know that making tortillas can seem like a little bit of work, but you will thank yourself, especially when you have some left to make quesadillas later. Saving the legs from the duck to make duck cassoulet, for me feels like a real win – luxurious meals to share and to sustain. The pineapple cakes are such a nice way to finish up. Tonka beans (a small jar will last ages) have a similar flavour to vanilla, cherry or almond, and paired with pineapple (somewhat surprisingly, perhaps, a winter fruit), bring some tropical sun to a chilly winter.

Which brings me to the last winter menu – **One to lie down after**. This is a traditional British Sunday roast with gravy and all the trimmings – just the way my family made it as I was growing up, and still makes it today. Chicken is the meat on offer, but that doesn't mean we have to forgo the Yorkshire puddings – giant, gorgeous ones that are far too good to be saved only for roast beef. Who makes the best Yorkshires in my family is the subject of many a good-humoured squabble – my nan and grandad have never settled their own claim to that crown. We bicker, too, about who gets the crispy ones and who gets the soft (I'm a soft girl myself). Sticky carrots and double-cooked roasties (extra fluffiness assured) are served up alongside, and not forgetting my favourite part: the mushy peas. Sweetened with a little bit of sugar (another tip from my grandad) and sumptuously soft, they are the green that completes the perfect roast. You could use the earlier menu's crumble for dessert, if you like, but I've gone for profiteroles – because this is a blow-out, have-to-lie-down Sunday roast, and it's winter and I love pastry.

Winter

Menu seven
This green and pleasant land

Remixes

Menu eight
The temper of saccharine

Remixes

Menu nine
One to lie down after

Remixes

Leek Pakoras *with* Shallot Chutney

Makes 16

40 minutes, plus soaking

For the shallot chutney

800g (1¾lb) banana shallots, skins on

800ml (1⅓ pints) boiling water from a kettle

4 tablespoons flavourless oil

6 garlic cloves

3 tablespoons caster (superfine) sugar

4 tablespoons sherry vinegar

a few thyme sprigs

For the pakoras

175g (6oz) gram flour

1 green chilli, finely chopped

1 teaspoon ground coriander

2 teaspoons garam masala

2 leeks, thinly sliced into rounds

a handful of coriander, leaves picked
and finely chopped

a small handful of mint, leaves picked
and finely chopped

1 teaspoon nigella seeds

500ml (16fl oz) flavourless oil, for
deep frying

salt and freshly ground black pepper

01 Make the chutney. Preheat the oven to 200°C (180°C fan/400°F/Gas 6). Place the shallots in a heatproof bowl and pour over the boiling water. Leave for 20 minutes, until the skins have softened. Remove the skins by cutting off the root end of the shallot and peeling off the first layer.

02 Heat the oil in a large ovenproof frying pan over a medium–high heat. Add the shallots and fry for 5–6 minutes, until they begin to brown. Add the garlic cloves and cook for a further 1–2 minutes, then add the sugar and reduce the heat to medium–low.

03 Once the sugar has begun to lightly brown (about 3–4 minutes), add the vinegar and 75ml (2½fl oz) of water. Add the thyme sprigs, then transfer the pan to the oven for 10–15 minutes, until the shallots are golden and sticky. ***To make the Shallot and Pea Bhuna (see page 128), transfer 7 shallots to an airtight container. Refrigerate for up to 4 days.***

04 While the shallots are baking, make the pakoras. Mix together the gram flour, chilli, ground coriander and garam masala in a bowl. Add the remaining ingredients, except the oil, and stir. Little by little, pour in 110ml (3¾fl oz) of water, mixing well between each addition to form a batter. Season with salt and pepper.

05 Pour the oil into a deep, heavy-based saucepan and heat it to 180°C (350°F) on a cooking thermometer, or until a cube of day-old bread sizzles and turns golden in 1 minute. (Alternatively, use a deep-fat fryer.) Four at a time, drop tablespoons of the batter into the oil, turning and frying for 3–4 minutes, until golden all over. Set aside to drain on kitchen paper while you fry the remainder. Serve straight away on a platter with the shallot chutney for everyone to help themselves.

Everything-but-the-chicken Pie

Serves 4

1 hour 20 minutes, plus cooling and chilling

3 Maris Piper potatoes, peeled and
    thinly sliced

4 parsnips, peeled and thinly sliced

4 carrots, peeled and thinly sliced

90ml (3fl oz) flavourless oil

200g (7oz) kale, thinly sliced

1 large leek, sliced into 1cm (½in) rounds

8 Brussels sprouts, thinly sliced

2 garlic cloves, thinly sliced

50g (1¾oz) dried stuffing mixture

75ml (2½fl oz) boiling water from a kettle

1 tablespoon unsalted butter (optional)

2 x 320g ready-rolled puff pastry sheets

1 egg yolk, beaten with 4 tablespoons
    whole milk, to glaze

salt and freshly ground black pepper

01 Bring a large saucepan of salted water to a boil. Add the potatoes, reduce the heat and simmer gently for 5 minutes to parboil. Remove the potatoes from the water into a bowl. Pat dry with kitchen paper.

02 Tip the parsnips and carrots into the water and parboil for 3 minutes. Transfer the vegetables to a separate bowl. ***To make the Chickpea Bake (see page 130), transfer one third each of the potatoes, parsnips and carrots to an airtight container. Refrigerate for up to 2 days.*** Discard the cooking water.

03 Heat the oil in a large frying pan over a medium heat. Add the kale, leek, sprouts and garlic and fry for 10–15 minutes, until softened and the kale begins to crisp very slightly on the edges. Remove from the heat.

04 Combine the stuffing and boiling water in a bowl until it is the texture of mashed potato. Add the butter (if using), stirring well to combine. Leave everything to cool for 30 minutes.

05 Line a baking tray with greaseproof paper. To assemble the pie, cut a 23cm-diameter (9in) disc from 1 pastry sheet (use a plate as a guide) and transfer it to the lined baking tray. Spread over the stuffing, leaving a 2.5cm (1in) border around the edge. Top with a layer of potatoes, then a layer of carrots, then parsnips, tightly packing each layer to keep it distinct. Spoon the cooked greens on top, moulding to create a domed top.

06 Cut a 26cm-diameter (10½in) disc from the second pastry sheet (roll it out a bit, if necessary) to create the lid. Brush the glaze around the border of the filled pastry base, then lay the lid over the top, smoothing it over the filling. Lightly press the pastry edges together to seal the pie.

07 Brush a little more glaze over the top of the pie and cut 2 steam holes in the lid. Refrigerate for 30 minutes to firm up. Meanwhile, preheat the oven to 210°C (190°C fan/415°F/Gas 6–7).

08 Brush the chilled pie with the remaining glaze and check the steam holes are still open. Bake for 35–40 minutes, until the pastry is deeply golden and flaky and the filling is piping hot. Serve straight away.

Brie *and* Chive Cauliflower Cheese

Serves 4

50 minutes

2 cauliflowers, broken into florets

2 tablespoons flavourless oil

½ teaspoon salt

1½ teaspoons freshly ground black pepper, plus extra to season

125g (4½oz) unsalted butter

125g (4½oz) plain (all-purpose) flour

500ml (16fl oz) whole milk

120g (4¼oz) good-quality brie, torn into pieces

80g (2¾oz) mature cheddar, grated

50g (1¾oz) cooking mozzarella, grated

a large bunch of chives, finely chopped

01 Preheat the oven to 220°C (200°C fan/425°F/Gas 7).

02 Place the florets into an ovenproof dish and drizzle with the oil. Sprinkle over the salt and 1 teaspoon of the pepper. Roast the cauliflower in the centre of the oven for 25 minutes, until there is some deep browning over the florets. Remove from the oven and set aside.

03 While the cauliflower is cooking, melt the butter in a large saucepan over a low heat. Tip in the flour and whisk to a smooth paste. Add the remaining black pepper and whisk for 3–4 minutes to cook out the flour. The mixture should be smooth and silky and come away easily from the bottom of the pan.

04 Gradually whisk in the milk, increasing your whisking speed to make sure no lumps form, then add all the cheeses. Leave the sauce, without whisking, over a low heat for 10 minutes, until warmed through, then increase the heat to medium–high and whisk again to melt the cheeses and form a thick sauce.

05 Pour half the sauce over the baked cauliflower, sprinkle over half the chives and mix well. Place the cauliflower cheese into the oven and bake for 15 minutes, until hot through and crispy on top. ***To make the Caramelized Onion and Roasted Garlic Mac 'n' Cheese (see page 129), transfer the remaining cheese sauce (about 200g/7oz) into an airtight container. Refrigerate for up to 3 days, or freeze for up to 1 month (defrost before using).*** Sprinkle the remaining chives over the baked cauliflower cheese and serve straight away.

Rhubarb, Orange *and* Vanilla Crumble

Serves 4

30 minutes

8 rhubarb stalks, cut into 3cm (1¼in) pieces
1 orange
90g (3oz/⅓ cup + 1 tablespoon) caster
       (superfine) sugar
2 teaspoons vanilla paste

For the crumble topping
150g (5½oz/1 cup) plain (all-purpose) flour
150g (5½oz) unsalted butter, cubed and
       chilled
4 tablespoons caster (superfine) sugar
4 tablespoons flaked almonds

01 Preheat the oven to 220°C (200°C fan/425°F/Gas 7). Line a baking tray with greaseproof paper.

02 Place the rhubarb in an ovenproof dish. Using a vegetable peeler, peel away the orange skin. Use a small knife to scrape away any white pith from the strips of skin. (You can zest the orange, but the flavour won't be as strong.) Put the orange peel into the baking dish with the rhubarb (eat the flesh), then spoon in the sugar, vanilla and 300ml (10fl oz) of water. Stir to combine. Bake in the centre of the oven for 20 minutes, until the rhubarb yields when pressed with the back of a spoon.

03 While the rhubarb is cooking, make the crumble. Place the flour, butter and sugar into a large mixing bowl and, using your fingertips, rub them together to create a breadcrumb-like texture. Add the almonds and mix to distribute evenly. Sprinkle the crumble on to the lined baking tray and bake it in the centre of the oven for 15–20 minutes, until golden. The mixture will still be slightly soft when you take it out – that's okay. As it cools, it will become more crunchy.

04 *To make the Rhubarb and Honey Yogurt Pots (see page 132), spoon 6 pieces of baked rhubarb into an airtight container. Refrigerate for up to 3 days.* Divide the remaining rhubarb pieces equally between 4 serving bowls. *For the topping for the Rhubarb and Honey Yogurt Pots, place 2 tablespoons of the crumble topping into an airtight container. Store at room temperature for up to 5 days.* Sprinkle the remaining crumble equally on top of the rhubarb in the bowls, then serve. *To make the Rhubarb Sorbet (see page 132), spoon the leftover juices from the baked rhubarb into an airtight container. Refrigerate for up to 5 days, or freeze for up to 1 month (defrost before using).*

SHALLOT AND
PEA BHUNA

A bhuna is probably the single most flavoursome dish you can make in relation to its time and effort. I also love the fact that so much about a bhuna is flexible: replacing the peas with papaya and tomatoes or prawns is my favourite mash-up. The addition of the sweet shallots here makes this remix quite special – try it for a Friday-night treat.

Serves 2-3   35 minutes

2 tablespoons flavourless oil

3 tablespoons ginger paste

3 tablespoons garlic paste

7 roasted shallots from Leek Pakoras with Shallot Chutney (see page 120)

2 teaspoons roasted curry powder

2 teaspoons garam masala

100ml (3½fl oz) boiling water from a kettle

1 tablespoon tomato purée

150g (5½oz) fresh or frozen peas

a generous handful of sugar snap peas (optional)

small flat breads, or roti, warmed, to serve

01 Heat the oil in a medium frying pan over a medium heat. Add the ginger and garlic pastes and cook for 3-4 minutes, until aromatic.

02 Use two forks to shred the roasted shallots, then add them to the frying pan. Cook for 3 minutes, then add the curry powder and garam masala and cook for 1 minute more to release the flavours. Add the boiling water.

03 Reduce the heat to low and cook the bhuna for 10-15 minutes, until thickened slightly and smelling delicious.

04 Add the tomato purée, peas, sugar snap peas (if using) and about 2 tablespoons of water. Simmer for 4-5 minutes, until the vegetables are tender, then serve straight away with warmed flat breads or roti on the side.

CARAMELIZED ONION AND ROASTED GARLIC MAC 'N' CHEESE

Whenever you are making a roux, you have an opportunity for mac 'n' cheese – so this remix is a no-brainer. I think there is very little that is as hunger-inducing as the sweet smell of roasted garlic – except perhaps the smell of caramelized onions. In that sense, then, this remix will have you chomping at the bit.

Serves 2-3   20 minutes

200g (7oz) dried pasta of choice
2 teaspoons flavourless oil
1 large red onion, finely chopped
4 garlic cloves, thinly sliced
200g (7oz) cheese sauce from **Brie and Chive Cauliflower Cheese (see page 123)**
a couple of handfuls of grated mature cheddar, to sprinkle (optional)
a handful of chives, finely chopped, to serve
salt

01 Bring a saucepan of salted water to a boil. Add the pasta and cook according to the packet instructions, until al dente.

02 Meanwhile, heat the oil in a large frying pan over a medium heat. When hot, add the onion and garlic and cook for 10-12 minutes, continuously moving them around the pan, until the garlic is lightly browned, but making sure neither the garlic nor the onion burn.

03 Once the pasta is almost cooked, add a ladleful of the pasta cooking water to the pan with the onion and garlic, then add the cheese sauce and stir quickly to combine. Add another ladleful of pasta cooking water to create a runny consistency.

04 Drain the cooked pasta and tip it into the frying pan with the sauce. Stir well to coat.

05 I enjoy this mac straight out of the pan just like this, but you can transfer it to a baking dish if you like, sprinkle with the grated cheddar and place under a preheated hot grill (broiler) for 5-6 minutes, until golden and crispy on top. Sprinkle generously with chives to serve.

CHICKPEA
BAKE

Much in the same way that I like to rest a frittata before I tuck in, I think this bake is best as a chilled wedge from the fridge (although it's good warm, too). I like to have it cold for lunch with a drizzle of tamarind or tomato chutney. It will keep, covered in the fridge, for up to 3 days.

Serves 8   1 hour, plus cooling

flavourless oil, for oiling the tin
1 onion, diced
10 cherry tomatoes, chopped
a handful of coriander (cilantro), leaves
    and stems chopped
2 teaspoons caster (superfine) sugar
2 heaped teaspoons medium curry powder
½ teaspoon ground cinnamon
1 x 400g can of chickpeas (garbanzos), drained
    and rinsed
reserved potatoes, carrots and parsnips
    from Everything-but-the-Chicken Pie
    (see page 122)
150g (5½oz) gram flour
salt and freshly ground black pepper

<u>01</u> Preheat the oven to 220°C (200°C fan/425°F/ Gas 7). Oil a deep, 20cm (8in) cake tin and set aside.

<u>02</u> Place the onion, tomatoes and coriander (cilantro) in a large bowl with the sugar. Season with salt and add the curry powder and cinnamon and mix well.

<u>03</u> In a separate bowl, combine the chickpeas (garbanzos) with the potatoes, carrots and parsnips. Add the gram flour and 300ml (10fl oz) of water with a generous seasoning of salt and pepper. Use a large spoon to mix everything together well, then tip it all into the cake tin and press down to create an even layer.

<u>04</u> Cover the cake tin with a lid or foil and bake for 30 minutes. Remove the lid and finish off uncovered for 20 minutes, until golden.

<u>05</u> Remove from the oven and leave to cool for at least 10 minutes before slicing into wedges to serve warm or cold.

RHUBARB AND HONEY YOGURT POTS

I like to keep my leftover glass food jars and make up these pots ready for the week ahead. Being able to go and get something from the fridge that I've lovingly put together and that's packaged up nicely makes me really feel like I've got it together! And it cuts down on the temptation to eat something quick that might not be as good for me.

Makes 2   5 minutes

6 pieces of baked rhubarb from Rhubarb, Orange and Vanilla Crumble (see page 126)
120ml (4fl oz) full-fat Greek yogurt
2 tablespoons runny honey
2 tablespoons crumble topping from Rhubarb, Orange and Vanilla Crumble, or shop-bought granola

01 Divide the rhubarb equally between two serving dishes and spoon 2 tablespoons of the yogurt into each. Add 1 tablespoon of runny honey per serving and top with the remaining the yogurt. Sprinkle over the crumble (or granola) topping to finish.

RHUBARB SORBET

This sorbet is basically already made once you've made the rhubarb crumble - all you have to do is add the orange juice, if you want to, and then stir it every few hours during the setting process. This is a nice recipe to make at the end of rhubarb season, as it will keep for a month in the freezer and you can go back and enjoy it even when you can't get your hands on any fresh rhubarb.

Serves 2-4   10 minutes, plus freezing

reserved juices from Rhubarb, Orange and Vanilla Crumble (see page 126)
juice of 1 orange, plus a few slivers of peel to serve (optional)
2 tablespoons flaked almonds, toasted (optional)

01 Pass the rhubarb juices through a sieve into a jug to remove any bits. Pour the juice into a freezerproof container and stir in the orange juice (if using).

02 Place the lid on the container and transfer the mixture to the freezer. Every 2-4 hours remove it from the freezer, take off the lid and give the sorbet mixture a good stir with a fork to break up the ice crystals. Replace the lid and return it to the freezer. Repeat this at least 4 times - the more repetitions you can make, the finer the final texture of your sorbet will be, so feel free to keep going.

03 To serve, scoop out the sorbet into bowls and sprinkle over a few toasted flaked almonds and slivers of orange peel, if you wish (it's equally delicious with or without - up to you!).

Swede Cake *with* Sweetcorn Ketchup

Serves 4

40 minutes, plus cooling and chilling

300g (10oz) swede, peeled and finely
    grated

4 tablespoons flavourless oil, plus extra
    for oiling the pan

1 onion, chopped

4 garlic cloves, chopped

150g (5½oz) sucuk sausage (chorizo or
    Chinese sausage also work very well),
    finely diced

250g (9oz) glutinous rice flour

2 tablespoons light soy sauce

½ teaspoon ground white pepper

½ teaspoon salt, plus extra to season

300ml (10fl oz) boiling water from a kettle

For the sweetcorn ketchup

3 tablespoons flavourless oil

1 leek, chopped

1 onion, chopped

1 x 340g can of sweetcorn, drained

150ml (5fl oz) single (light) cream

1½ tablespoons caster (superfine) sugar

To serve

2 spring onions (scallions), finely sliced

2 tablespoons chilli oil

01 Pour 200ml (7fl oz) of water into a large saucepan and add the swede and a sprinkling of salt. Bring the water to a boil, then reduce the heat to a simmer and cook for 10–15 minutes, until the swede is softened but not mushy.

02 In the meantime, heat the oil in a large frying pan over a medium heat. Add the onion, garlic and sausage and fry for 10 minutes, until the onion is lightly browned and aromatic.

03 While the onion, garlic and sausage are cooking, place the rice flour, soy sauce, white pepper, and salt into a mixing bowl and stir in 250ml (9fl oz) of water, mixing to form a completely smooth batter.

04 Add the sausage mixture to the cooked swede, turn off the heat, then add the rice-flour mixture, stirring quickly to combine. Place the mixture into a cake tin or baking dish that will fit inside a steamer basket and smooth the top of the mixture.

05 Add the boiling water to the steamer pan and place the steamer on top. Steam the "cake" for 10 minutes, until firm to the touch. (If you don't have a steamer, use a colander with a foil lid.) Remove from the steamer, leave to cool, then chill (covered) for at least 2 hours.

06 Meanwhile, make the ketchup. Pour the oil into a large frying pan over a medium heat. When hot, add the leek and onion, season generously with salt and sweat for 3–4 minutes, until everything starts to soften.

07 Add the drained sweetcorn and cook for 2 minutes, then add the cream, sugar, and 150ml (5fl oz) of water. Simmer for 2 minutes, then turn off the heat. *__To make the Sweetcorn and Pumpkin Chowder (see page 142), transfer 250g (9oz) of the sweetcorn mixture to an airtight container. Refrigerate for up to 4 days. (To save washing-up, I like to make the chowder straight away, letting it simmer while I eat dinner.)__* Using a hand-held stick blender, blitz the remaining mixture to a smooth consistency. Transfer to a bowl and leave to cool.

08 To serve the swede cake, remove it from the fridge and cut it into 2cm (¾in) squares. Lightly oil a frying pan and warm it over a medium–high heat. When hot, add the squares and fry for 2–3 minutes on each side, until browned (do this in batches if necessary).

09 Plate up the swede cake squares, covering them generously with sliced spring onions (scallions) and chilli oil. Serve with the sweetcorn ketchup alongside (if you have any ketchup leftover, you can add it to the mixture you've reserved for the chowder, if you wish).

Honey *and* Spice Roasted Duck

Serves 4

3 hours 20 minutes

2 cinnamon sticks

5 cloves

3 star anise

1 teaspoon black peppercorns

1 teaspoon fennel seeds

10 spring onions (scallions), trimmed

1 duck (about 1.2–1.5kg/2lb 10oz–3lb 3oz),
    innards removed

1 teaspoon Chinese 5-spice

75ml (2½fl oz) runny honey

salt

lime wedges, to serve

01 Preheat the oven to 180°C (160°C fan/350°F/Gas 4).

02 Place the cinnamon, cloves, star anise, peppercorns and fennel seeds into a baking tray and add the spring onions (scallions). Set aside.

03 Using a fork, pierce lots of small holes in the skin of the duck, taking care not to pierce all the way through to the flesh. Use a sharp knife to cut a criss-cross pattern into the skin. Pat the skin dry with some kitchen paper and place the duck, skin side down, into a cold frying pan, then place the pan over a medium heat. Fry the skin until the fat begins to melt and the skin browns. (For super-crispy skin, put another cold pan on top of the duck and press down to allow the fat to render more easily.) Once one side is browned, turn the duck to brown the other side.

04 Transfer the duck to the baking tray, on top of the spices and spring onions. Sprinkle over the 5-spice and season generously with salt. Pour any fat from the frying pan over the duck, then cover with foil.

05 Roast the duck in the centre of the oven for 2 hours, then baste with the liquid from the bottom of the baking tray. Increase the heat to 220°C (200°C fan/425°F/Gas 7) and roast for a further 1 hour, uncovered, to crisp up the skin. In the last 10 minutes, drizzle over the honey and increase the heat to 250°C (230°C fan/500°F/Gas 9) for super-crispy skin. Remove from the oven. *To make the Duck Cassoulet (see page 144), remove the duck legs, allow them to cool and then wrap them in foil. Refrigerate for up to 3 days.* Allow the duck to rest for 20 minutes or so, before serving with lime wedges for squeezing over.

Corn Tortillas and Spring Onion Salsa

Makes 20

45 minutes

For the salsa

½ cucumber, chopped into small pieces

10 mixed-colour tomatoes, quartered

1 red chilli, finely chopped

4 spring onions (scallions), sliced into thin
    rounds

2 roasted red (bell) peppers from a jar,
    chopped into small pieces

4 tablespoons white vinegar

1 tablespoon caster (superfine) sugar

¼ teaspoon sesame oil

juice and finely grated zest of 2 limes

a small handful of coriander (cilantro)
    leaves, finely chopped

a small handful of mint leaves, finely
    chopped

For the tortillas

200g (7oz/scant 1¾ cups) PAN flour
    (preferably) or masa harina (fine
    cornflour/corn starch)

2 teaspoons baking powder

300ml (10fl oz) boiling water from a kettle

100g (3½oz/⅔ cup) plain (all-purpose) flour

01 Make the salsa. Combine the cucumber, tomatoes, chilli, spring onions (scallions) and (bell) peppers in a serving bowl. Add the vinegar, sugar, sesame oil and lime juice and zest and stir to combine, then add the coriander (cilantro) and mint and stir again. Set aside (it will keep for 1 day in an airtight container in the fridge).

02 Make the tortillas. Place the masa harina into a large bowl. Using a wooden spoon, stir in the baking powder. Pour in the boiling water, stirring quickly to make a thick dough. Sprinkle the plain (all-purpose) flour into the bowl and knead to incorporate (take care – it will be hot). Portion the dough into 20 equal-sized balls.

03 Place each ball between two pieces of greaseproof paper and, if you have a tortilla press, pass it through. If you don't have a press, place a heavy object, such as a heavy pan, on top of each ball to flatten it. Remove the object and roll out the tortilla using a rolling pin until it is as thin as possible (aim for about a 10cm/4in disc).

04 Stack the tortillas as you go, separating them with the sheets of greaseproof paper.

05 To cook, place a large, non-stick frying pan over a high heat. Cook the tortillas, 2 or 3 at a time, on one side for 1–2 minutes, pressing down with a spatula, until very lightly browned with brown spots, then flip and cook for 30 seconds, until the other side has brown spots, too. Remove the cooked tortillas to a large container and cover with a lid to keep them warm as you cook the remainder. ***To make the Corn and Red Pepper Quesadillas (see page 146), transfer 6 cooked tortillas to an airtight container. Refrigerate for up to 4 days.*** Serve with the duck and the salsa alongside. (You can use any leftover salsa for the quesadillas on page 146, too.)

Tonka Bean *and* Pineapple Cakes

Serves 4

1 hour, plus resting and cooling

400g (14oz) fresh pineapple flesh, cut into
   1cm (½in) pieces
140g (5oz/scant ⅔ cup) caster (superfine)
   sugar, plus 3 tablespoons for the dough
1 tonka bean
250g (9oz) unsalted butter, cubed, plus
   extra for greasing
350g (12oz/2⅓ cups) plain (all-purpose)
   flour
1 egg yolk
3 tablespoons whole milk

To decorate (optional)

150g (5½oz) white chocolate, chopped
50g (1¾oz) dried pineapple, finely chopped

01 Place the pineapple in a medium saucepan with the sugar and 1 tablespoon of water, then grate in the tonka bean. Stir well to make sure the sugar is evenly distributed. Place the pan over a medium–low heat and cook for 10 minutes, until the pineapple is sticky and all of the sugar has dissolved. Turn off the heat and tip the sticky pineapple into a bowl. Cover with cling film and place in the fridge to cool.

02 Meanwhile, place the butter, the 3 tablespoons of sugar and all the flour into a mixing bowl and rub them together with your fingertips to a breadcrumb-like texture. Add the egg yolk and the milk and mix with your hands to a soft and pliable, but not sticky dough (if the dough is too sticky, add an extra tablespoon of flour and then knead until the dough is smooth). Knead the dough for 5 minutes, then leave it to rest for 10 minutes.

03 While the dough is resting, grease a 12-cup muffin tray with butter and place it in the fridge. Preheat the oven to 220°C (200°C fan/425°F/Gas 7).

04 Once the dough has rested, roll it into a log shape about 20cm (8in) long and 5cm (2in) thick. Divide it into 14 equal pieces, then cover the pieces with a clean tea towel to stop them from drying out while you make the cakes.

05 Take 1 piece of dough and roll it into a ball. Place the ball into your palm and use the fingers of your other hand to press down to form a rough disc. Place 1 teaspoon of the pineapple mixture into the centre of the disc (don't overfill), then pull the dough up around the pineapple

mixture to seal the filling inside. Use your fingertips to smooth over the dough. Place the pineapple cake into one of the compartments of the prepared muffin tray and, one by one, make a further 11 in the same way to give 12 in total. Flatten the remaining 2 dough discs slightly into cookies and place them on a baking sheet lined with greaseproof paper.

06 Bake the cakes and the dough disks for 25 minutes, until lightly browned. Remove them from the oven and leave them to cool in the tin/on the baking sheet for 10 minutes, then transfer to a wire rack to cool completely. ***To make the Tonka Bean Custard with Baked Plums (see page 147), place the 2 baked cookies into an airtight container. Store at room temperature for up to 3 days.***

07 You can eat the cakes like this if you like, but I like to decorate them with some melted white chocolate and a sprinkling of dried pineapple. Place the white chocolate in a microwave-safe bowl and melt it on medium power in 5-second bursts, stirring between each burst. Drizzle the chocolate over the cooled pineapple cakes and finish with the dried pineapple pieces.

SWEETCORN AND PUMPKIN CHOWDER

The word chowder instantly makes me feel warm inside. This recipe may not include the more traditional fish ingredients, but it is nonetheless one of those stick-to-the-ribs comfort foods that really gives you everything you need in a cosy autumn meal. I heartily recommend serving it up with a big hunk of your favourite bread.

Serves 2–3   50 minutes

250g (9oz) sweetcorn mixture from Swede Cake with Sweetcorn Ketchup (see page 134)
500ml (16fl oz) hot vegetable stock
1 Maris Piper potato, peeled and chopped into 2cm (¾in) pieces
1 small pumpkin or squash, peeled, deseeded and chopped into 2cm (¾in) pieces
salt and ground white pepper
2 spring onions (scallions), sliced, to serve
hunks of your favourite bread, to serve

FOR THE PICKLED ONIONS (OPTIONAL)
2 red onions, thinly sliced
75ml (2½fl oz) red wine vinegar

FOR THE CROÛTONS
1 small baguette
1 garlic clove, crushed
1 tablespoon chilli oil

01 Place the sweetcorn mixture in a large saucepan and add the vegetable stock, potato and pumpkin or squash.

02 Add a generous seasoning of salt and a touch of white pepper, place over a medium heat and bring to a boil. Reduce the heat to a strong simmer, put the lid on the pan and cook for 30 minutes. Then, remove the lid, reduce the heat to low and simmer gently for 15 minutes, until the vegetables are completely soft and collapsing.

03 While the chowder is cooking, make the pickled onions (if using). Place the onion slices in a small bowl and pour over the vinegar. Season with salt, then leave the onions to macerate for 15 minutes, until they are bright pink. Transfer to a sterilized jar and seal with a lid (any leftovers will keep in the fridge for up to 7 days).

04 Make the croûtons. Preheat the oven to 200°C (180°C fan/400°F/Gas 6). Tear the baguette into small pieces into a bowl and add the crushed garlic and chilli oil. Mix well to make sure that all of the bread is covered in the seasoning. Transfer to a baking tray and toast in the oven for 7–10 minutes, until crispy. Remove from the oven and set aside until the chowder is ready.

05 Ladle the chowder into warmed bowls and top each serving with a few croûtons and a sprinkling of spring onion (scallion) slices. Top with a few slices of drained pickled onions, too, if you wish, and serve with hunks of bread. (If you have croûtons left over, freeze them for another time – simply pop them into a moderate oven for 5–10 minutes to crisp up again as they defrost.)

DUCK CASSOULET

A whole duck can be a little bit pricey, so using the legs in this remix means that from just one duck you get two absolutely delicious and impressive meals. This recipe serves two, but it's easy to make it stretch to serve four: simply shred the meat from the duck legs instead of adding the legs whole, and/or add a couple of extra sausages.

Serves 2   35 minutes

1 tablespoon flavourless oil
1 onion, chopped
2 tablespoons garlic paste
2 herby sausages (optional)
2 rosemary sprigs
2 thyme sprigs
1½ tablespoons tomato purée
1 tablespoon white wine vinegar
1 x 400g can of haricot beans, drained and rinsed
1 chicken stock cube
**2 duck legs from Honey and Spice
   Roasted Duck (see page 136)**
hunks of sourdough, to serve

01 Heat the oil in a large frying pan over a medium-high heat. When hot, add the onion and the garlic paste and fry for 10 minutes, until the onion is lightly browned.

02 Split open the sausages (if using) and remove the meat from the middle, breaking it into small pieces and adding it to the pan with the onion. Discard the sausage skins.

03 Add the rosemary and thyme sprigs, stirring everything to combine, then cook for a further 3 minutes. Once the sausagemeat is browned, add the tomato purée and vinegar and cook for a further 2 minutes, then tip in the haricot beans. Stir to combine.

04 Crumble in the chicken stock cube and add about 150ml (5fl oz) of water, then place the duck legs into the pan, nestling them just underneath the beans. Place the lid on the pan, reduce the heat to medium-low and cook for 15 minutes, until piping hot throughout. Serve with hunks of sourdough for dipping.

CORN AND RED PEPPER QUESADILLAS

Having leftover tortillas is quite rare in our house, but assuming you kept the extra aside, as suggested, quesadillas are the way to go. This remix is my favourite combo for the filling (I think I might be addicted to cheddar), but you can add any fillings or cheese that you like. Oaxaca or Monterey Jack might be more traditional, for example; or red leicester, for a bit of colour.

Serves 2   20 minutes

1 x 160g can of sweetcorn, drained
2 roasted red (bell) peppers from a jar, finely
    chopped
1 red chilli, finely chopped
60g (2oz) mature cheddar, grated
**6 cooked tortillas from Corn Tortillas and Spring
    Onion Salsa (see page 137)**
1 teaspoon flavourless oil
**leftover salsa from Corn Tortillas and Spring
    Onion Salsa, to serve (optional)**

<u>01</u> Combine the sweetcorn, (bell) peppers, chilli and cheddar in a mixing bowl.

<u>02</u> Place 3 tortillas on your work surface and spoon one third of the cheesy mixture on to each, spreading it out evenly but leaving a 2cm (¾in) border around the edge. Top each with another tortilla.

<u>03</u> Heat the oil in a large frying pan over a medium heat.

<u>04</u> Using a spatula, gently transfer 1 quesadilla into the frying pan and cook for 3–4 minutes, until the underside begins to brown and the cheese inside starts to melt. Carefully flip over the quesadilla and cook for a further 2 minutes, until browned. Remove from the pan and keep warm while you cook the remaining quesadillas. (You can cook more than one at once, if your pan is big enough.)

<u>05</u> To serve, slice the quesadillas into wedges. If you have any leftover salsa, spoon this over the top.

TONKA BEAN CUSTARD
WITH BAKED PLUMS

*When you've gone to the trouble of sourcing an
unusual ingredient, such as tonka beans (online is
a good start), it's always good to have alternative
ways to use them. I first came across tonka bean
custard in my first job as a chef – thanks Ricardo!
– and I've made it ever since. Here, the shortbread
dough discs from the pineapple cakes offer a
contrast of texture to the baked plums and custard.*

Serves 2   20 minutes

FOR THE PLUMS
3 plums, destoned and quartered
2 tablespoons caster (superfine) sugar
**2 baked cookies from Tonka Bean and Pineapple
    Cakes (see page 140), crumbled**

FOR THE CUSTARD
250ml (9fl oz) shop-bought vanilla custard
½ tonka bean
3 tablespoons whole milk

01 Preheat the oven to 200°C (180°C fan/
400°F/Gas 6).

02 Bake the plums. Place the plums in a small
baking dish with the sugar and stir well. Transfer
them to the oven and bake for 15 minutes, until
softened and sticky.

03 Meanwhile, make the custard. Pour the custard
into a small saucepan, grate in the tonka bean and
pour in the milk. Whisk everything together, then
place over a medium heat for 5 minutes, until the
custard is bubbling and thickened. Keep warm.

04 Once the plums are cooked, remove from the
oven and spoon them into serving bowls. Pour over
the warm custard and sprinkle with the crumbled
cookies. (You can even remix the remix: transfer any
leftover plums to an airtight container, top with
custard and leave to cool, then refrigerate to enjoy
the following day.)

Chorizo *and* Fennel Jam on Toast *with* Blue Cheese

Serves 4

35 minutes

200g (7oz) spicy chorizo sausage, skin removed

4 tablespoons flavourless oil

1 onion, finely chopped

6 garlic cloves, finely chopped

1 teaspoon fennel seeds

2 tablespoons golden caster (superfine) sugar

4 thin slices of seeded baguette

60g (2oz) blue cheese (I like Oxford blue), crumbled

2 teaspoons finely chopped chives, to serve (optional)

01 Pull apart the chorizo into small pieces and place the pieces into a bowl.

02 Heat the oil in a large frying pan over a medium heat. When hot, add the onion and garlic and cook for 10–12 minutes, until the garlic begins to brown and smell aromatic.

03 Add the fennel seeds and cook for 3 minutes, then add the chorizo. Cook, stirring, for 2–3 minutes, until the chorizo starts to release its oils. ***To make the Chorizo and Pepper Orzo (see page 158), transfer 2 heaped tablespoons of the mixture to an airtight container. Refrigerate for up to 5 days.*** Add the sugar to the remainder in the pan and stir well, then add 100ml (3½fl oz) of water, bring to a boil and boil for 2 minutes, to make a sticky and thick jam.

04 Remove the jam from the heat and transfer it to a sterilized jar. It's best served warm, but it will store refrigerated for 7–10 days, just make sure that you use a clean spoon every time you scoop some out.

05 Preheat the grill (broiler) to high. Toast the bread slices under the grill for 1–2 minutes on both sides, until crispy. Transfer to a serving plate and spoon the warm chorizo jam on top. Sprinkle over the blue cheese, and the chopped chives (if using). Serve straight away.

Lemon *and* Garlic Roasted Chicken

Serves 4

1 hour 50 minutes, plus cooling and resting

1 extra-large chicken (about 1.8–2.5kg/ 4–5½lb)

2 carrots, sliced

1 leek, sliced

1 onion, sliced into half moons

10 garlic cloves

a large handful of rosemary sprigs

a large handful of thyme sprigs

½ tablespoon black peppercorns

1 lemon, thinly sliced

4 tablespoons flavourless oil

salt and freshly ground black pepper

For the gravy

2 tablespoons flavourless oil

1 onion, halved and sliced

1 tablespoon tomato purée

4 tarragon sprigs, leaves picked

1 chicken stock cube

1 teaspoon cornflour (corn starch) dissolved in 2 teaspoons water

01 Spatchcock the chicken: turn it upside down and cut 2 long slits down the middle, either side of the spine. Remove the spine and freeze it to turn into stock at a later date. Turn the chicken over and press it with your palm to flatten it out. (You could ask your butcher to do this for you, if you prefer.)

02 Place all the sliced vegetables, the garlic herbs and the peppercorns, and a generous seasoning of salt, into a large saucepan (one that will hold the whole chicken) and place the chicken, breast side down and shaped to fit, on top. Add enough water to cover the chicken.

03 Stir gently to make sure that the water loosens the vegetables at the bottom so that they don't burn, then cover with a lid or foil and bring the liquid to a boil over a high heat. Immediately reduce the heat to low and simmer for 30 minutes, until the chicken turns white and opaque and is partly cooked.

04 Lay the slices of lemon in a baking tray and, using a pair of tongs, remove the chicken from the pan and place it, breast side up, on top of the lemon slices. Replace the lid on the pan and leave the vegetables to simmer for a further 30 minutes.

05 Leave the chicken to cool for 20 minutes in the baking tray, then pat dry with kitchen paper. Preheat the oven to 250°C (230°C fan/500°F/Gas 9).

06 Once the vegetables have been bubbling away for 1 hour altogether, increase the heat to high and remove the lid. Boil rapidly until the liquid has reduced by half (about 15 minutes). Strain the stock through a sieve into a jug and set aside 300ml (10fl oz) for the gravy (freeze any extra stock for another time and discard the contents of the sieve).

07 Pour the oil over the chicken, spreading it to coat. Season generously with salt and pepper. Roast in the centre of the oven for 20 minutes, until cooked through. Allow to rest in a warm place for about 20 minutes before carving. ***To make the Bang Bang Chicken Salad (see page 159) and the Chicken and Ginger Broth with Noodles and Spring Onions (see page 160), transfer 200g (7oz) of the white or dark meat to an airtight container. Once you've carved the remainder of the chicken for your main meal, wrap the carcass in foil. The reserved meat and the carcass will keep in the fridge for up to 3 days.***

08 While the chicken is resting, make the gravy. Heat the oil in a large saucepan over a medium heat. Add the onion and cook for 10 minutes, until completely softened and beginning to caramelize. Add the tomato purée and cook for 1 minute, then add the tarragon leaves and cook for a further 1 minute. Pour in the reserved vegetable stock and crumble in the stock cube. Bring to a simmer and simmer for 10 minutes, stirring occasionally. Whisk in the cornflour (corn starch) and stir the gravy for 2–3 minutes, until thickened. Remove it from the heat and pour it into a warmed gravy boat if you're ready to serve straight away (otherwise, keep warm as necessary).

Classic Sunday Lunch Sides

Serves 4

1 hour 20 minutes

For the roasties

120ml (4fl oz) flavourless oil

6 large, floury potatoes, each cut into
    4 large pieces

2 garlic cloves

salt and freshly ground black pepper

For the roasted carrots

2 tablespoons flavourless oil

8 carrots, peeled and sliced on the diagonal
    into 2cm (¾in) chunks

¼ star anise

1 tablespoon runny honey

finely grated zest of 1 orange

salt and freshly ground black pepper

For Grandad's mushy peas

200g (7oz) dried marrowfat peas, soaked
    overnight in water and 1 tablespoon
    bicarbonate of soda (baking soda)

1 teaspoon salted butter

1 tablespoon caster (superfine) sugar

For the Yorkshire puddings

100ml (3½fl oz) flavourless oil

8 eggs

280g (9½oz/1¾ cups + 1 tablespoon)
    plain (all-purpose) flour

400ml (14floz) whole milk

ground white pepper

01 Preheat the oven to 220°C (200°C fan/425°F/Gas 7).

02 Make the roasties. Pour the oil into a large baking tray and place it in the oven until hot (about 15 minutes).

03 Meanwhile, bring a large saucepan of salted water to a boil. Add the potatoes and boil them for 10 minutes, then drain in a colander. Leave them in the colander to dry out for about 10 minutes.

04 Remove the hot baking tray from the oven and tip in the potatoes, being careful not to splash yourself with hot oil. Return the tray to the oven and roast the potatoes for 25 minutes, then turn the potatoes over and roast for a further 30 minutes, until golden and crispy. *To make the Bubble and Squeak (see page 163), transfer 4 roast potatoes to an airtight container. Refrigerate for up to 3 days.*

05 While the potatoes are roasting, also make the roasted carrots. Drizzle half the oil into a baking tray. Add the carrots, season with salt and pepper and drizzle over the remaining oil. Use a fine grater to grate over the star anise. Roast the carrots (in the oven with the potatoes) for 25 minutes, then turn them over and roast for a further 25 minutes, until caramelized and tender. Once cooked, remove them from the oven and drizzle over the honey and sprinkle over the orange zest. *To make the Bubble and Squeak, transfer 10 carrot pieces, to an airtight container. Refrigerate for up to 3 days.*

06 Meanwhile, make the mushy peas. Rinse the soaked peas in cold water to remove the bicarbonate of soda (baking soda).

07 Place the peas into a medium saucepan and cover with water. Bring to a boil over a high heat, then reduce the heat and simmer for 45 minutes–1 hour, until the water has evaporated and the peas are completely soft. Add the butter and sugar and stir well. Keep warm until you are ready to serve. ***To make the Bubble and Squeak, transfer 4 tablespoons of the peas to an airtight container. Refrigerate for up to 3 days.***

08 To make the Yorkshire puddings, pour the oil equally into the hollows of a 12-cup Yorkshire pudding or muffin tin and place it into the oven to get very hot (about 15 minutes).

09 Meanwhile, make the batter. Crack the eggs into a large mixing bowl, then whisk in the flour, a little at a time, until completely smooth. Season with salt and white pepper, then gradually add the milk, whisking all the time to make sure that no lumps form, until the batter is thick and smooth. Transfer half the batter to a jug and leave it to rest for at least 10 minutes while the oil heats up. (You can make the batter a day before, if you like, and keep it in the fridge overnight.) ***To make the Mediterranean Toad in the Hole (see page 164), pour the remaining half of the batter into an airtight container. Refrigerate for up to 3 days.***

10 To cook the Yorkshires, carefully remove the hot tin from the oven. Place it on a heatproof surface and evenly pour in the remaining Yorkshire batter so that it comes two-thirds of the way up the sides of each hollow. Return the tin to the oven and cook for 20–25 minutes, until the Yorkshires are risen and golden brown.

11 Take the baked Yorkshires straight out of the tin, so that they don't soak in any extra oil. ***To make the Yorkshire Pudding Sundaes (see page 164), set aside 4 puddings. Leave to cool, then pop them into a freezer bag. Refrigerate for up to 2 days, or freeze for up to 1 month (heat up from frozen).*** (You could bake the Yorkshires in advance, if you prefer – simply put them back into the oven 3–5 minutes before serving your roast to heat up again.)

Chocolate Profiteroles *with* Orange Blossom Custard

Serves 4

1 hour 15 minutes, plus cooling and chilling

120ml (4fl oz) whole milk

120g (4¼oz) unsalted butter

1 teaspoon caster (superfine) sugar

¼ teaspoon salt

155g (5¾oz/1 cup) plain (all-purpose) flour

4 eggs

For the orange cream filling

3 egg yolks

3 teaspoons caster (superfine) sugar

3 teaspoons cornflour (corn starch)

300ml (10fl oz) whole milk

2 teaspoons orange blossom essence
    (or use vanilla paste, if you prefer)

For the chocolate glaze

100g (3½oz) milk chocolate, broken up

50g (1¾oz) 70% dark (bittersweet)
    chocolate, broken up

1 teaspoon unsalted butter

100ml (3½fl oz) double (heavy) cream

01 Preheat the oven to 220°C (200°C fan/425°F/Gas 7). Line a large baking tray with greaseproof paper.

02 Pour the milk into a medium saucepan along with 120ml (4fl oz) of water. Add the butter, sugar and salt and place the pan over a medium–low heat, until the butter has melted. Increase the heat to medium–high and bring the liquid to a gentle boil. Immediately turn off the heat and tip in the flour, stirring vigorously with a wooden spoon for 1–2 minutes to make a smooth batter.

03 Transfer the batter to a mixing bowl and spread it up the inside of the bowl to help it cool. Leave to cool for 4 minutes.

04 Meanwhile, crack the eggs into a jug and whisk with a fork to break them up.

05 Once the batter is just slightly warm, add the eggs, one third at a time, beating well between each addition. Leave to cool completely. ***To make the Gruyère Gougères (see page 166), transfer half the batter to an airtight container. Refrigerate for up to 3 days.***

06 Place the remaining batter into a large piping (pastry) bag and twist the top. Hold the piping bag above the lined baking tray and pipe 12 small mounds (about 3–4cm/1¼–1½in in diameter), spacing them well apart to allow for expansion during baking. Lightly dab each mound with a wet finger to smooth the top. Bake in the centre of the oven for 25–30 minutes, until golden brown and crisp. Leave to cool on the tray for 10 minutes, then transfer to a wire rack to cool completely.

07 Meanwhile, make the filling. Whisk together the egg yolks, sugar and cornflour (corn starch) for 2 minutes to combine. Place the milk into a medium saucepan over a medium–high heat and bring to a boil. Immediately remove the pan from the heat and add the essence. Slowly pour the mixture over the eggs, whisking the whole time to a smooth custard.

08 Tip the custard back into the pan and place it over a medium–low heat. Stir thoroughly for about 5–8 minutes, until the cream is thick enough to briefly hold its shape if you drag a spatula across the bottom of the pan. Pour the filling into a bowl, cover the surface with cling film to prevent a skin forming, and chill. Once cold, spoon the cream into a disposable piping bag and cut a small hole in the tip.

09 Slice the top off each choux bun. Pipe the cream into the bottom sections. Set the filled buns aside, without the lids, while you make the glaze.

11 Place both chocolates in a heatproof bowl with the butter and set aside. Heat the cream over a low heat to just boiling. Pour the hot cream over the chocolates and leave for 5 minutes. Whisk to fully melt the chocolates and combine the mixture until silky smooth.

12 Dip the top of each bun lid into the glaze to coat, then place it, glaze up, over a filled bottom. Transfer to a serving plate to set. ***To make the Chocolate and Coffee Mousse Pots (see page 167), measure 100g (3½oz) of the remaining glaze and use it straight away (while it is still soft) – the recipe will take only 5 minutes.***

CHORIZO AND
PEPPER ORZO

I once made a batch of chorizo jam and took it on a first date. The date didn't work out, but I did get a message a few months later about how good the jam was! Apart from how quick it is to make, the thing I love about this pasta dish is the balance of flavours. Fennel and chorizo are smoky and aromatic, a combination that is the perfect foil for the piquant cheese.

Serves 2   20 minutes

200g (7oz) dried orzo pasta

1 tablespoon unsalted butter

½ teaspoon freshly ground black pepper

30g (1oz) manchego (or other strong, hard cheese), grated, plus extra to serve

2 heaped tablespoons chorizo mixture from Chorizo and Fennel Jam on Toast with Blue Cheese (see page 148)

salt

01 Bring a medium saucepan of salted water to a boil. Add the orzo and cook according to the packet instructions, until al dente.

02 About 5 minutes before the pasta is cooked, melt the butter in a large frying pan over a high heat. Add the black pepper and cook for 1 minute, then add the grated manchego (or other cheese) and the chorizo mixture.

03 Once the pasta is almost cooked, add a ladleful of the pasta cooking water to the frying pan and continue cooking over a high heat for about 2 minutes, until the liquid has reduced by half. Reserve 1 more ladleful of the pasta water in a cup to the side.

04 Drain the cooked pasta and tip it into the frying pan. Stir well to coat in the sauce, adding the reserved pasta cooking water to give you enough liquid, if necessary (if you don't need it, discard the water).

05 To serve, divide the pasta between the serving bowls and sprinkle over a little extra manchego (or other cheese), if you want to be especially decadent.

BANG BANG CHICKEN SALAD

While I'm sure you've had leftover chicken salads before and your heart might be sinking a bit at the thought of another, let me assure you – this one is far from boring. The dressing is the secret – you'll love it so much that you'll make it again and again... each time loving it a little more.

Serves 2   15 minutes

1 teaspoon sesame oil
1 tablespoon crunchy peanut butter
2 teaspoons sweet soy sauce, or light soy
    sauce mixed with 1½ teaspoons caster
    (superfine) sugar
1 teaspoon runny honey or caster (superfine) sugar
2 teaspoons rice vinegar or other vinegar
100g (3½oz) Lemon and Garlic Roasted Chicken
    (see page 150), shredded
2 carrots, peeled and sliced into matchsticks
2 spring onions (scallions), sliced into thin strips
1 red (bell) pepper, deseeded and sliced into thin
    strips
a handful of mixed leaves, shredded

FOR THE SALAD DRESSING
2 teaspoons rice vinegar (or other vinegar)
2 teaspoons sweet soy sauce, or light soy sauce
    mixed with 1½ teaspoons caster (superfine)
    sugar
1 teaspoon sesame oil

TO SERVE (OPTIONAL)
a sprinkling of dried chilli flakes
a sprinkling of crushed unsalted roasted peanuts

01 Mix together the sesame oil, peanut butter, soy sauce, honey or sugar and vinegar in a small jug to form a sauce.

02 Place the shredded chicken into a frying pan over a high heat. Pour over the sauce and cook, stirring occasionally to prevent the sugars from burning, for 6–8 minutes, until the sauce thickens and darkens.

03 Meanwhile, in a separate bowl, mix together all the ingredients for the salad dressing.

04 Once the chicken is ready, toss the sliced vegetables and leaves in the bowl with the salad dressing and divide it equally between your serving plates. Portion the hot chicken on top. If you like, finish with a sprinkling of chilli flakes and crushed roasted peanuts.

CHICKEN AND GINGER BROTH WITH NOODLES AND SPRING ONIONS

Even just the idea of a chicken noodle soup fills me with feelings of wholesomeness. Over the past few years, I have become increasingly waste conscious and, although there's always more I could do, this recipe certainly makes inroads in easing my woes. There is something quite special about using up all the bits and pieces of your roasted chicken. That said, if you don't have any leftover chicken, replace the boiled water in the recipe with good-quality chicken stock for the easiest and most delicious of dinners.

Serves 2   1 hour

1 roasted chicken carcass from Lemon and Garlic Roasted Chicken (see page 150)
500ml (16fl oz) boiling water from a kettle
4 x 2.5cm (1in) slices of peeled fresh ginger
1 chicken stock cube (optional)
2 eggs
3 nests of dried egg noodles
a large handful of greens (longstem broccoli, spinach and kale are all great, trimmed as necessary)
100g (3½oz) chicken meat from Lemon and Garlic Roasted Chicken
salt and freshly ground black pepper
4 spring onions (scallions), finely chopped, to serve
a sprinkling of black and white sesame seeds, to serve (optional)

01 Place the chicken carcass into a large saucepan over a medium heat. Pour in the boiling water and add the sliced ginger. Put the lid on the pan (or cover with foil) and simmer gently for 30 minutes to start a broth.

02 Remove the lid and simmer the broth for a further 20 minutes, until the liquid has slightly reduced. Taste, then season with salt and pepper. If the broth needs some extra flavour, crumble in the chicken stock cube. If not, remove the chicken carcass, pull off any meat still attached to the bones and place the meat back into the broth. Discard the carcass.

03 Wash the eggs under warm water to clean them thoroughly. Increase the heat under the pan to a boil and place the eggs, noodles and greens into the broth. Boil for 6–7 minutes, then remove the eggs using tongs or a slotted spoon and place them into a bowl of cold water. Turn off the heat.

04 Divide the noodles between two serving bowls. Add the chicken meat and ladle in the broth. Peel and halve the eggs and place them on top. To serve, sprinkle with the spring onions (scallions), and with the sesame seeds (if using).

BUBBLE AND SQUEAK

When I was young, bubble and squeak was a weekly treat. The whole family would go to my nan's house on a Sunday for a traditional roast, then on Monday my sister and I would have all the leftovers made into bubble and squeak for dinner. At the time, I never thought of it as eating leftovers – as far as I was concerned, it was the most exciting part of yesterday's lunch. Brown sauce on the side is my grandad's influence – I can't have it without.

Serves 1–2   20 minutes

**4 roast potatoes from Classic Sunday Lunch
    Sides (see page 154)**
**10 pieces of carrot from Classic Sunday
    Lunch Sides**
**4 tablespoons mushy peas from Classic
    Sunday Lunch Sides**
2 tablespoons plain (all-purpose) flour
1 large egg
2 tablespoons flavourless oil

TO SERVE
1–2 eggs, plus a little flavourless oil for frying
    (optional)
brown sauce
1–2 spring onions (scallions), finely sliced

<u>01</u> Place the potatoes in a large mixing bowl and squash them with the back of a large spoon to break them up. Add the carrots and crush those, too, then add the peas and flour. Mix everything together, then add the egg and mix again until the egg is fully mixed through and all the ingredients are combined.

<u>02</u> Heat the oil in a large frying pan over a medium-high heat, then add 4 large tablespoons of the bubble-and-squeak mixture to the pan, forming them into rough patties with the spoon once they are in the pan. Fry for 4 minutes on each side, until crisped-up and browned all over. Transfer the patties to a serving plate and keep warm.

<u>03</u> To serve, fry the eggs (if using) as you like them, then place them on top of the patties, drizzle with a generous amount of brown sauce and finish with a sprinkling of the spring onions (scallions).

MEDITERRANEAN TOAD-IN-THE-HOLE

Whenever I make Yorkshire puddings, I double the recipe to make enough for a "toad" in the week. A traditional toad uses sausages, but this one uses Mediterranean vegetables in their place. In fact, though, you can make toad-in-the-hole with any number of ingredients you have to use up – tomatoes, mushrooms and broccoli are all good additions, too.

Serves 2   50 minutes

135ml (4½fl oz) flavourless oil
4 garlic cloves, thinly sliced
4 sundried tomatoes, chopped
1 small courgette (zucchini), roughly chopped
1 green (bell) pepper, deseeded and roughly chopped
1 onion, roughly chopped
reserved Yorkshire pudding batter from Classic Sunday Lunch Sides (see page 154)

01 Preheat the oven to 210°C (190°C fan/415°F/ Gas 6–7). Pour two thirds of the oil into a large baking tray and place in the centre of the oven to heat up (about 15 minutes).

02 Meanwhile, heat the remaining oil in a large frying pan over a medium-high heat. When hot, add the garlic and fry for about 3–4 minutes, until just softened and aromatic. Add the sundried tomatoes, courgette (zucchini), (bell) pepper and onion and fry for 4–5 minutes, until just softened.

03 Remove the hot baking tray from the oven and tip in the vegetables from the frying pan. Pour the Yorkshire pudding batter over the vegetables and bake in the centre of the oven for 30 minutes, until puffed up and golden. Serve straight away.

YORKSHIRE PUDDING SUNDAES

When I first heard about the notion of eating Yorkshire puddings with jam (it's a thing), I was skeptical. Then, I thought about it. Leftover Yorkshire batter makes good pancakes, so it makes a lot of sense that the leftover Yorkshires themselves could be used as cups of deliciousness to hold sweet treats – like ice cream, chocolate sauce and sprinkles.

Serves 4   10 minutes

4 Yorkshire puddings from Classic Sunday Lunch Sides (see page 154)
8–12 scoops of ice cream of your choice (I think salted caramel works particularly well)
chocolate sauce (optional)
sugar sprinkles (optional)

01 Preheat the oven to 220°C (200°C fan/425°F/ Gas 7).

02 Place the Yorkshire puddings on a baking tray in the centre of the oven to warm through for 3–5 minutes, then remove from the oven and transfer into individual serving dishes. Slightly tear open each pudding to make a cavity for the ice cream, if necessary.

03 Scoop in your choice of ice cream, then finish with chocolate sauce and sprinkles, if you wish. Serve straight away.

GRUYÈRE GOUGÈRES

I like to cut open these cheesy buns and stuff them with ham (and perhaps more cheese – but I've held back in this remix) and have the most adorable little gougère morsels for lunch or as a getting-home-from-work snack. You can use any cheese you like, but a dry cheese works best.

Makes 12   50 minutes, plus cooling

**reserved choux batter from the Chocolate
    Profiteroles with Orange Blossom Custard
    (see page 156)**
40g (1¼oz) mature cheddar, finely grated
slices of ham, to serve

01 Preheat the oven to 200°C (180°C fan/400°F/Gas 6). Remove the choux batter from the fridge, transfer it to a bowl and stir to loosen it. Line a large baking tray with greaseproof paper.

02 Fold the cheese through the pastry, making sure that it's fully incorporated into the dough. Then transfer the pastry to a disposable piping (pastry) bag and cut off the tip about 2.5cm (1in) from the end of the bag.

03 Pipe 12 small mounds (about 5cm/2in in diameter) of choux pastry all over the lined baking tray, spacing them well apart to allow the buns to expand as they bake (or, make éclair shapes, about 6cm/2½in long, if you prefer). Dab the top of each bun with a wet finger to flatten and smooth the tops.

04 Bake the buns in the centre of the oven for 25–30 minutes, until golden brown and crisp. Leave to cool on the tray for 10 minutes, then transfer to a wire rack to cool completely. To serve, slice each bun in half and stuff it with ham for a light lunch.

CHOCOLATE AND
COFFEE MOUSSE POTS

*I think coffee beautifully brings out the flavour
of chocolate, and turning leftover chocolate glaze
into little mousses for the end of a busy day (or to
share, but who are we kidding?) is about as good
an idea as there can be. If coffee isn't your thing,
though, feel free to use the zest of an orange or a
couple of drops of peppermint extract instead.
The important thing is that you have little
chocolate pots to get you through the week.*

Makes 4   5 minutes, plus chilling

1 tablespoon ground coffee
**100g (3½oz) glaze from Chocolate Profiteroles
    with Orange Blossom Custard (see page 156)**
100ml (3½fl oz) double (heavy) cream

01 Put the ground coffee and the glaze in a small
saucepan and stir over a low heat for 1 minute, until
the coffee is incorporated and the glaze has melted.
Remove from the heat.

02 In a bowl, whip the cream to stiff peaks, then
add it, one third at a time, to the coffee–chocolate
mixture, stirring between each addition until you
have a smooth, fully incorporated ganache.

03 Spoon the ganache into 4 small ramekins
and cover with cling film. Refrigerate for at
least 2 hours – or for up to 4 days, if you wish –
before serving.

Spring

There's nothing that I don't absolutely love about spring. The changing of the seasons lends its magic to those beautiful fresh-blue-sky days that then pair themselves with star-studded clear nights. You'll find me looking up, wrapped up against the chilly reminder of winter, but with all the hope of new beginnings. It's this mood that is very much reflected in the food of this chapter. The starters are dainty and delicious to share with friends and family over a glass of something cold and refreshing – but each yields enough left over to make some more substantial dinners throughout the week. The mains are zesty, with all the freshness and hope of spring – and the desserts just keep on giving. Perfect.

Treasures of the farmers' market is a menu full of springtime treats that you can pick up at local Saturday stalls with added cheerful banter thrown in for free. Aubergines come into their best at the end of spring. I first tried the Spicy Aubergine and Sesame Eggs at Bao London and I just knew I had to make my own. Who doesn't love the subtle flavours of tangy orange with chicken? To me, this is the epitome of a springtime main. However, it's the Cherry and Almond Cake that takes the star turn in this menu. I think the method of cooking the butter and citrus in a pan first is genius – it saves on the clearing up compared with traditional cake-making methods, and for all my love of cooking, I can't stand making more mess than is necessary. Cherries are a summer fruit, really, but the heady scent of this cake reminds me of the glorious blossom that is so redolent of springtime – so spring it is.

I wanted to include a vegan feast in the book that anyone and everyone would be thrilled to eat. The second menu in this chapter – **That which grows on the earth** – is that. The Crispy Fried Oyster Mushrooms are like a better version of chicken wings, soaking up all that smoky paprika flavouring in the coconut milk. I used to make cashew-nut spring rolls – the main – as a vegan option for a Sunday roast in a restaurant where I was head chef, and the customers loved them. I've rounded off this menu with a rice pudding – with a homemade praline spread that is every bit as good as the filling in my favourite chocolate bar and gives you plenty of leftovers for smearing over toast during the week. For me, that's perfection.

Spring's final menu – and the final one in the book – is called **Feast of all worlds**. Seeing as spring is a season in which we traditionally celebrate new beginnings, it seems an apt time to discover and celebrate diversity in some of my favourite world cuisines (and I like the irony of finishing the book with the notion of something new and fresh). First up are my Manchego Croquettes with Quince Jam, inspired by Spanish tapas and a superb way to use up the last of the winter quinces, just as they come to the end of their best. Vampire Lamb is my version of a traditional British roast lamb, but it's the Mapled Cream Kale with Paneer that provides the exotic twist, reminiscent as it is of the food of East Asia. This side also yields one of my most cherished leftover recipes – Peshwari Swirls. Miso is a traditional Japanese seasoning and in this menu I've used it to give extra silkiness and umami flavour to the humble (but always delicious) banoffee pie. You'll have enough miso caramel left over to make yourself a banana and caramel shake during the week, too – American diner meets Japanese fermented beans in springtime... who'd have thought?

Spring

Spicy Aubergine *and* Sesame Eggs

Serves 4

35 minutes

7 eggs

3 tablespoons flavourless oil

1 aubergine (eggplant), sliced into
matchsticks

3 spring onions (scallions), thinly sliced

1 tablespoon ginger paste

1 tablespoon garlic paste

1 tablespoon dried chilli flakes

1 tablespoon white vinegar

1 tablespoon light soy sauce

¼ teaspoon sesame oil

30g (1oz) mature cheddar or parmesan,
grated, to serve

01 Bring a large saucepan of water to a boil over a medium–high heat. Gently add the eggs and cook for 6 minutes to hard boil. Drain the pan – if you like a really runny yolk, fill the pan with cold water; if you prefer your yolk firmer, just set the eggs aside (they will go on cooking as they cool).

02 Pour the flavourless oil into a frying pan over a high heat. Fry the aubergine (eggplant) for 10–12 minutes, until browned, then remove from the pan and set aside. Add the spring onions (scallions), ginger paste, garlic paste and chilli flakes to the pan. Fry for 3–4 minutes, until the spring onions have softened. Add the vinegar, soy sauce and sesame oil and cook for a further 2–3 minutes, then add back the aubergine and mix well. Reduce the heat to low and cook for 2–3 minutes, until the mixture has melded.

03 Peel and halve 4 of the eggs and arrange them on a serving plate. ***To make the Japanese Egg Sando (see page 183), place the remaining 3 eggs in an airtight container. Refrigerate for up to 3 days.*** Top each peeled egg half with a spoonful of the aubergine mixture, then sprinkle the grated cheese on top to serve.

Roasted Garlic, Orange *and* Thyme Chicken

Serves 4

1 hour

4 bone-in chicken legs

1 teaspoon salt

a large handful of thyme sprigs, leaves
  picked, plus extra sprigs for roasting
  and optional extra leaves to serve

100g (3½oz) unsalted butter, at room
  temperature

3 garlic cloves

½ teaspoon freshly ground black pepper

3 oranges

1 tablespoon flavourless oil

01 Remove the chicken from the fridge at least 1 hour before roasting to allow it to come up to room temperature, place it into a roasting tin and sprinkle it with the salt. Preheat the oven to 230°C (210°C fan/450°F/Gas 8).

02 In a food processor, blitz the thyme leaves, butter, garlic and black pepper until fully combined. (Or, you can use a pestle and mortar to crush together the thyme, garlic and pepper or you can chop them very finely, then mash the mixture into the butter.) **To make the Thyme Butter and Soft-scrambled Eggs on Toast (see page 184), place 1 teaspoon of the blended butter in an airtight container. Refrigerate for up to 1 week.**

03 Grate the zest from 1 of the oranges into the mixture, add the oil and blend (or mix) again to a smooth paste.

04 Using gloves, completely cover the chicken legs in the butter mixture. Slice the zested orange and 1 further orange into 3 slices each and place the slices in the roasting tin with a few extra thyme sprigs.

05 Roast the chicken in the centre of the oven for 25 minutes, then reduce the heat to 200°C (180°C fan/400°F/Gas 6) and roast for a further 25 minutes, until the legs are cooked through and the juices run clear.

06 Remove the chicken from the oven and zest over the final orange (save the segments to eat later). Add a sprinkling of extra thyme leaves, if you like, before serving.

Baked Mustardy Leeks
with Cheddar

Serves 4

45 minutes

500ml (16fl oz) double (heavy) cream
150g (5½oz) mature cheddar, grated
4 teaspoons wholegrain mustard
4 leeks, sliced into 1cm (½in) rounds
30g (1oz) parmesan (or use mature
     cheddar), grated
salt and freshly ground black pepper

01 Preheat the oven to 220°C (200°C fan/425°F/Gas 7).

02 In a large bowl, combine the double (heavy) cream, cheddar and mustard, and season well with salt and pepper.

03 Tip the leeks into the bowl, turning them to coat as evenly as possible. Transfer the mixture to a baking dish.

04 Sprinkle over the parmesan (or cheddar) and bake in the centre of the oven for 35–40 minutes, until the top is golden brown. ***To make the Leek and Spring Onion Mac 'n' Cheese (see page 185), transfer half the leeks (200g/7oz) to an airtight container. Refrigerate for up to 3 days.*** Leave to rest for 5 minutes before serving.

Cherry *and* Almond Cake

Serves 4

55 minutes, plus cooling

For the cherries and cherry syrup

500g (1lb 2oz) cherries, pitted

1 tablespoon vanilla paste

400g (14oz/generous 1¾ cups) caster (superfine) sugar

For the cake

250g (9oz) unsalted butter, plus a little extra to grease the tin

250g (9oz/1 cup + 2 tablespoons) caster (superfine) sugar

1 teaspoon vanilla paste

juice and finely grated zest of 1 orange, lemon or lime

250g (9oz/2½ cups) ground almonds

50g (1¾oz/⅓ cup) plain (all-purpose) flour

2 eggs

½ tsp baking powder (optional)

icing (confectioners') sugar, for dusting

01 Preheat the oven to 220°C (200°C fan/425°F/Gas 7).

02 Place the cherries into a medium saucepan with the remaining cherry ingredients and 90ml (3fl oz) of water. Simmer over a low heat for about 15 minutes, until the sugar has dissolved and the cherries are soft but not mushy. Remove from the heat and set aside.

03 To make the cake, grease a 20cm (8in) square cake tin with butter and line the bottom and sides with greaseproof paper. Heat the butter and sugar together in a large saucepan over a low heat, stirring occasionally, for about 4–5 minutes, until melted, then add the vanilla and citrus juice and zest.

04 Tip in the almonds and flour and cook for a further 2–3 minutes, until the mixture thickens slightly. Turn off the heat and leave to cool for a couple of minutes. One at a time, whisk in the eggs until fully combined, then tip in the baking powder (if using) and whisk until smooth.

05 Pour the cake batter into the prepared cake tin and spoon in 6 tablespoons of the cherries on top (don't worry if your cherries sink to the bottom during baking – the cake will still be delicious). Bake in the centre of the oven for 25 minutes, until golden and a skewer inserted into the centre comes out clean. If it's not quite ready at the first test, cover with foil and bake for an extra 5 minutes. Leave to cool in the tin.

06 Dust with icing (confectioners') sugar, then cut into slices to serve. Spoon another couple of tablespoons of cherries on top of each serving. ***To make the Cherry Iced Tea and the Mascarpone and Cherry French Toast (see page 186), spoon at least 4 tablespoons of the cherry syrup and the remaining cherries into a sterilized jar. Refrigerate for up to 1 week.***

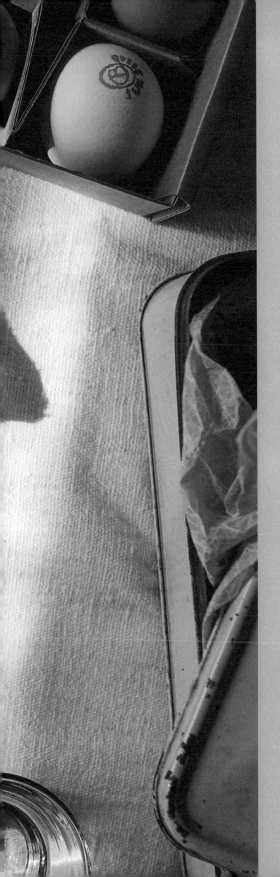

JAPANESE EGG SANDO

I'm not sure I can be convinced there is a better sandwich than the egg sando. For the effort that you put in and the deliciousness you get out, for me, it is unmatched. There's something so visually appealing about having the whole egg in the middle, too.

Serves 2   10 minutes

4 slices of white bread (preferably milk bread)
3 hard-boiled eggs, shelled, from Spicy Aubergine and Sesame Eggs (see page 174)
4 tablespoons Japanese mayonnaise

01 Lay 2 slices of bread on the work surface in front of you. Slice one of the eggs in half and place one half, yolk side down, into the middle of each slice.

02 Put the remaining eggs in a bowl and add the mayonnaise. Using a fork, break up the eggs into small pieces, combining them with the mayo as you go.

03 Spoon equal amounts of the egg mayonnaise on top of and around the egg half on each slice of bread, spreading it to the edges in an even layer.

04 Sandwich with the remaining bread slices and press together to seal. Slice each sandwich in half, to serve.

THYME BUTTER AND SOFT-SCRAMBLED EGGS ON TOAST

I grew up eating microwaved scrambled eggs and never really thought of them as something that could be a real meal – and, honestly, I still don't really mind them that way as a sidekick to a cooked breakfast. It wasn't until I became a chef and learned that you can judge a good restaurant purely by the way it treats its eggs that I realized slow-cooked scrambled eggs is a game-changer. The remix use of the thyme butter in these eggs takes them to another level (but, of course, unsalted butter will work perfectly well, too).

Serves 2   10 minutes

4 eggs
1 teaspoon thyme butter from Roasted Garlic, Orange and Thyme Chicken (see page 176)
2 slices of your choice of bread, toasted, then buttered if you wish
a sprinkling of sea salt
a sprinkling of thyme leaves (optional)

01 Crack the eggs into a medium saucepan, then add the thyme butter and use a wooden spoon to gently break up the eggs. Place over a low heat and stir continuously, until the eggs start to cook. I like my eggs cooked to a medium-soft texture, which will take about 5–8 minutes; if you like yours firmer, cook them over a medium heat for about 5–6 minutes.

02 Spoon the eggs on top of the toasted (and buttered, if you like) bread and sprinkle over some sea salt and thyme leaves to finish, if you like. Serve straight away.

LEEK AND SPRING ONION MAC 'N' CHEESE

Unsophisticated as it may sound, mac 'n' cheese might just be my favourite pasta dish of all time – partly because it presents endless possibilities for flavour combinations. This one is so easy (you've already got the sauce for a start), but if you want to give it some more jazz, try adding cubes of chorizo just before baking or a sprinkling of toasted garlic breadcrumbs. For me, though, it makes a satisfying midweek supper just as it is.

Serves 2   40 minutes

200g (7oz) dried spiral or elbow macaroni
a knob of unsalted butter
½ teaspoon freshly ground black pepper
6 spring onions (scallions), sliced into
    1cm (½in) pieces
2 tablespoons plain (all-purpose) flour
200ml (7fl oz) whole milk
**200g (7oz) Baked Mustardy Leeks with Cheddar
    (see page 179)**
40g (1½oz) mature cheddar, grated (optional)
salt

01 Preheat the oven to 200°C (180°C fan/ 400°F/Gas 6).

02 Bring a large saucepan of salted water to a boil. Add the pasta and cook according to the packet instructions until al dente.

03 Meanwhile, place the butter and black pepper in a shallow, ovenproof saucepan (this helps save on washing up later – otherwise use a regular saucepan and transfer to an ovenproof dish when indicated) and allow the butter to melt over a low heat. Add three-quarters of the spring onions (scallions) and cook for 2–3 minutes, until slightly softened.

04 Add the flour and whisk to a smooth paste (a roux). Cook for 2–3 minutes to cook out the floury flavour, then season with salt. Whisking all the time, pour in the milk until you have a lump-free sauce, then continue to whisk for a further 1 minute. Whisk in the leeks to combine.

05 Drain the cooked pasta and add it to the sauce, stirring to coat. If you haven't been using an ovenproof pan, transfer the mac and cheese to a baking dish now.

06 Sprinkle over the remaining spring onions, and finish with a final flourish of cheese, if you like. Bake for 20–25 minutes, until bubbling and golden. Serve straight away.

CHERRY ICED TEA

I would be lying if I said I didn't base my days around the delicious treats that I'm going to have in it. Knowing I have a little jar of leftover cherry syrup in the fridge just for this cherry iced tea makes me giddy. And, the remix is so simple it practically makes itself.

Serves 1   5 minutes

1 regular tea bag
100ml (3½fl oz) boiling water from a kettle
2 tablespoons cherry syrup from Cherry and Almond Cake (see page 180)
juice of 1 lemon (optional)
a small handful of ice cubes

01 Place your tea bag into a heatproof glass and pour over the boiling water and the cherry syrup. Leave the tea bag to sit for 3 minutes, then squeeze it out and discard it. Leave the tea to cool.

02 Add the lemon juice (if using), then add the ice cubes and top up the glass with cold water. Stir with a long spoon and enjoy!

MASCARPONE AND CHERRY FRENCH TOAST

I know this remix may fall for a few extras (mascarpone and brioche or challah, for example), but I think it's worth adding them to the weekly shop, purely as an act of self-love – a sweet treat to help see you through the difficult days (or celebrate the good ones).

Serves 2   10 minutes, plus soaking

1 large egg, lightly beaten
5 tablespoons whole milk
½ teaspoon ground cinnamon
2 tablespoons cherry syrup from Cherry and Almond Cake (see page 180), plus optional extra to serve
2 slices of brioche or challah bread
2 tablespoons mascarpone or double (heavy) cream
flavourless oil, for frying
a few cherries from Cherry and Almond Cake

01 Put the egg, milk, cinnamon and 1 tablespoon of the cherry syrup into a large bowl and mix well. Add the slices of bread, leave them for 1 minute, then turn them over, letting them soak up the liquid.

02 Mix the remaining cherry syrup into the mascarpone or double (heavy) cream to combine.

03 Place a large frying pan over a medium heat. Add a little oil, then fry the bread slices for 2–3 minutes on each side, until lightly caramelized.

04 Transfer the French toast to serving plates, drizzle over the mascarpone or cream, and top with a few extra cherries, and a final drizzle of syrup, if you wish.

Crispy Fried Oyster Mushrooms
with Umami Ketchup

Serves 4

45 minutes, plus resting

For the mushrooms

150g (5½oz) rice flour

2 teaspoons garlic powder

2 teaspoons onion powder

2 teaspoons sweet smoked paprika

200ml (7fl oz) full-fat coconut milk

16 oyster mushrooms

500ml (16fl oz) flavourless oil,
    for deep frying

2 spring onions, finely sliced, to serve
    (optional)

For the umami ketchup

4 tablespoons flavourless oil

150g (5½oz) shiitake mushrooms

1 onion, chopped

4 smoked garlic cloves

1 tablespoon tomato purée

1 tablespoon brown miso

1 tablespoon sherry vinegar

1 tablespoon light soy sauce

1 tablespoon maple syrup, plus extra
    to serve

1 x 400g (14oz) can of chopped tomatoes

01 First, make the ketchup. Heat the oil in a large frying pan over a high heat. When hot, add the shiitake mushrooms, onion and garlic and fry for 8–10 minutes, until golden. Add the purée and miso and mix well.

02 Leave the mixture to cook for 1 minute, then add the vinegar, soy sauce and maple syrup and cook for 30 seconds more, stirring all the time. Add the tomatoes and 150ml (5fl oz) of water, bring to a simmer and leave for 5 minutes, until broken down. Pour the mixture into a heatproof jug and blitz with a hand-held stick blender to a smooth and silky consistency. Set aside to cool.

03 For the mushrooms, tip the rice flour into a large mixing bowl and stir in 1 teaspoon each of the garlic powder, onion powder and paprika. Set aside. In a separate bowl, combine the remaining garlic powder, onion powder and paprika with all the coconut milk to form a batter.

04 Dip the oyster mushrooms into the batter, then into the flour to coat. Using your hands, gently squeeze to push the flour into all of the crevices. Once coated, place each mushroom on to a greaseproof-lined baking tray. Leave for 10 minutes to allow the batter to set slightly.

05 Meanwhile, heat the 500ml (16fl oz) of oil in a deep, heavy-based saucepan to about 180°C (350°F) on a cooking thermometer, or until a cube of day-old bread sizzles and turns golden within 1 minute. (Alternatively, use a deep-fat fryer.) Deep-fry the mushrooms, a few at a time, for about 2–3 minutes, until golden and crispy. Scoop out each batch to a bowl lined with kitchen paper while you fry the remainder.

06 Transfer the mushrooms to a plate and drizzle with maple syrup and sprinkle with spring onions (if using). Serve with some umami ketchup for dipping. ***Transfer the remaining ketchup to an airtight container to enjoy with the Cheddar and Rice Flour Fritters (see page 196). Refrigerate for up to 3 days. Or freeze it in ice-cube trays to add an umami hit to bolognese or other sauces.***

Black Garlic
and Cashew Nut
Roast Rolls

Makes 8

50 minutes

90ml (3fl oz) flavourless oil, plus extra
    for brushing

2 red onions, diced

150g (5½oz) cashews

2 garlic cloves, thinly sliced

1 x 400g can of black beans, drained
    and rinsed

10 black garlic cloves

1 x 400g can of chickpeas (garbanzos),
    drained, liquid reserved

3 tablespoons maple syrup

3 teaspoons coconut amino (optional)

90g (3oz) plain (all-purpose) flour

1 x 550g packet of spring roll pastry
    (16 sheets)

01 Heat the oil in a large frying pan over a medium–high heat. Add the onions, cashews and garlic and fry for 4–5 minutes, stirring occasionally, until the mixture is lightly golden.

02 Add the black beans and black garlic to the pan and cook for 1–2 minutes, then add the chickpeas (garbanzos), maple syrup and coconut amino (if using). Reduce the heat to medium–low and cook for 10 minutes, until the chickpeas collapse when you press them with a spoon. Turn off the heat.

03 Preheat the oven to 220°C (200°C fan/425°F/Gas 7).

04 Mix together the flour with 4 tablespoons of water to create a paste.

05 Lay a sheet of pastry on the work surface with a long edge closest to you. Add 3 tablespoons of the chickpea mixture along the long side of the pastry, leaving enough border that when the pastry is folded over the filling, it will fully encase it.

06 Brush all the edges with the flour paste, roll the flap of pastry closest to you over the filling, then fold in the edges to seal. Roll the filled pastry away from you to wrap it up and seal fully. Place a second sheet of pastry on the work surface and wrap for a second time, sealing the edges with the paste again. Repeat until you have 8 double-wrapped rolls. ***To make the Za'atar and Cashew Spaghetti (see page 198), transfer the remaining filling to an airtight container. Refrigerate for up to 3 days.***

07 Lightly brush the rolls with oil and place them on a baking tray lined with greasproof paper. Bake them in the centre of the oven for 20–25 minutes, until golden and cooked through. (Alternatively, heat 500ml/16fl oz oil in a deep-fat fryer to 180°C/350°F and deep-fry the rolls for 3–4 minutes.) Serve 1 or 2 rolls per person, depending on appetite. Freeze any leftover rolls for up to 1 month (reheat from frozen).

Truffled Aubergine *with* Crispy Savoy

Serves 4

40 minutes, plus cooling

2 aubergines (eggplants)
2 teaspoons truffle oil
½ head of savoy cabbage
3 tablespoons flavourless oil
2 tablespoons granulated or caster
    (superfine) sugar
salt and freshly ground black pepper

01 Preheat the oven to 200°C (180°C fan/400°F/Gas 6).

02 If you have a gas hob, set a burner to a high flame, spear an aubergine (eggplant) on a fork or skewer and place it into the flame, turning occasionally, for 4–5 minutes, until it is blackened and charred on the outside. Transfer to a baking tray and repeat for the second aubergine. Place the baking tray in the oven and roast the charred aubergines for 15 minutes, until soft. (If you don't have a gas burner, simply roast the aubergines, whole, for 30 minutes, until soft.)

03 Remove from the oven and, when cool enough to handle, peel off the outer skins, then place the aubergine flesh into a food processor with the truffle oil. Season with salt and pepper and blend until smooth. ***To make the Smoky Aubergine Flat Bread (see page 195), spoon 6 tablespoons of the aubergine purée into an airtight container. Refrigerate for up to 3 days.*** Set the remainder aside.

04 Using a peeler, shred the cabbage very thinly (or use a sharp knife to slice the cabbage into thin strips).

05 Heat half the oil in a large frying pan over a high heat. When hot, place half the cabbage into the pan – taking care as it will spit. Toss the cabbage in the oil, allowing it to become crispy and lightly browned on the edges, then transfer it to a bowl lined with kitchen paper. Repeat for the remaining oil and shredded cabbage.

06 Tip all the cabbage into a clean bowl and sprinkle the sugar over the top. Season with salt and toss to coat.

07 Spoon the reserved smoked aubergine on to a serving plate and top with the crispy cabbage to serve.

Praline Rice Pudding

Serves 4

35 minutes

For the praline spread

100g (3½oz) blanched hazelnuts

80g (2¾oz) caster (superfine) sugar

50g (1¾oz) vegan white chocolate, grated, plus extra to serve (optional)

80ml (2¾fl oz) hazelnut milk

For the rice pudding

100g (3½oz) short grain pudding rice

70g (2¼oz) caster (superfine) sugar

500ml (16fl oz) hazelnut milk

½ teaspoon vanilla paste

01 Preheat the oven to 200°C (180°C fan/400°F/Gas 6).

02 For the praline spread, place the hazelnuts on to a baking tray and pop them in the oven for 10–12 minutes, until deeply golden.

03 Meanwhile, start the rice pudding. Place the rice and sugar in a large saucepan. Pour over the hazelnut milk and add the vanilla, stirring once to combine. Pop the pan over a medium–low heat, bring the liquid to a simmer and simmer for 25 minutes, until the rice begins to thicken. Then, turn off the heat.

04 While the rice is cooking, finish the spread. Set aside 5 of the roasted hazelnuts for decoration. Place the remainder into a food processor with the sugar, and the white chocolate (if using). Pulse until you have a thick, dry paste. Add the hazelnut milk and blend until smooth and combined. Transfer the spread to a sterilized jar.

05 Spoon the rice pudding into bowls and add a spoonful of the praline spread. ***To make the Bueno Toast (see page 199), reserve at least 2 tablespoons of the spread. Refrigerate for up to 1 week.*** Chop the reserved hazelnuts and sprinkle these over the top to serve, along with extra grated white chocolate, if you wish.

SMOKY AUBERGINE
FLAT BREAD

This is a perfect working-from-home lunch in that it's pretty much all assembly. You don't even have to warm through the aubergine if you don't want to – just take your favourite flat bread and dunk abundantly. The smoky aubergine reminds me of eating mezze somewhere warm and relaxing, providing me with a momentary, dreamy respite from the busy-ness of the real world.

Serves 2   5 minutes

6 tablespoons aubergine purée from Truffled Aubergine with Crispy Savoy (see page 191)
1 large flat bread or naan
1 red onion, very thinly sliced
30g (1oz) soft goat's cheese or vegan cream cheese
mixed leaf salad, to serve (optional)

01 Preheat the grill (broiler) to medium–high.

02 Spread the aubergine purée all over the flat bread or naan, then top with an even layer of onion slices. Dot around the cheese.

03 Place the flat bread or naan under the grill for 3–4 minutes, until the cheese is melty and the onion lightly cooked. Serve the flat bread, just as it is, or with a mixed leaf salad, if you wish.

CHEDDAR AND RICE FLOUR FRITTERS

Okay, I know – rice flour will last about for ever if properly sealed in a kitchen cupboard, but this is a great way to use it up. And, besides, you have your leftover umami ketchup, too. Don't be put off by how simple these little fritters look – they are absolutely bursting with flavour and make an excellent snack, and an equally excellent side to any meal that needs a carby accompaniment.

Serves 3–4   20 minutes

100g (3½oz) rice flour
300ml (10fl oz) boiling water from a kettle
3 spring onions (scallions), thinly sliced
100g (3½oz) mature cheddar, grated
90ml (3fl oz) flavourless oil
salt and freshly ground black pepper
leftover umami ketchup from Crispy Fried Oyster Mushrooms with Umami Ketchup (see page 188), to serve (optional)

01 Tip the rice flour into a large mixing bowl and quickly pour in the boiling water, whisking to make the mixture as smooth as possible (there may be a few lumps – this is fine). Add the spring onions (scallions), season with salt and pepper and allow the mixture to cool for 5 minutes.

02 Add the cheddar and use a spoon to mix everything together.

03 Divide and roll the mixture into 12 golf-ball-sized balls, then gently flatten them out in the palm of your hand. Set aside on a baking tray lined with greaseproof paper.

04 Heat the oil in a non-stick frying pan over a medium–high heat. In two batches, place the fritters into the pan, frying them for 1–2 minutes each side until browned. (If they stick to the pan, leave them for a moment longer as they will free themselves once they're cooked.) Set the first batch aside to drain on kitchen paper while you could the remainder. Serve as they are for a mid-afternoon treat, or alongside breakfast for a decadent alternative to hash browns.

ZA'ATAR AND CASHEW SPAGHETTI

I confess – sometimes I just eat the leftover filling for the cashew nut rolls standing over the pot when I make it. But let's pretend for a moment that I am able to exercise some self-control: this recipe is my absolute go-to remix for that filling. If you don't have any za'atar, try a sprinkling of dried thyme in its place, or even a grating of any cheese you have milling about in the fridge.

Serves 2   15 minutes

120g (4¼oz) dried spaghetti
**leftover filling from Black Garlic and Cashew
    Nut Roast Rolls (see page 190)**
2 teaspoons za'atar
juice of 1 lemon (optional)
salt

01 Bring a large saucepan of salted water to a boil. Add the spaghetti and cook according to the packet instructions, until al dente.

02 Once the pasta is almost cooked, place a frying pan over a medium heat. Add a ladleful of the pasta cooking water to the frying pan along with the leftover filling. Stir well to combine.

03 Using tongs, transfer the cooked spaghetti to the pan with the sauce and stir to coat.

04 Transfer the pasta to serving plates and finish with a sprinkling of za'atar, and the lemon juice (if using).

BUENO TOAST

During busy weeks, our house pretty much relies on meals that involve toast. At breakfast, having something like the delicious hazelnut spread in the fridge can make you feel like a king or queen at the very start of the day. With a coffee on the side, too, who cares that it's Wednesday and you have a to-do list as long as your arm?

Serves 2   5 minutes

2 slices of your choice of bread
unsalted butter, for spreading
2 tablespoons hazelnut praline spread from
    Praline Rice Pudding (see page 194)
25g (1oz) white chocolate, grated, to serve

01 Toast the bread to your liking, then spread it with butter.

02 Spread 1 tablespoon of the hazelnut praline spread on each slice and finish with a grating of white chocolate.

Manchego Croquettes
with Quince Jam

Serves 4

2½ hours, plus cooling

For the quince jam

3 quinces

juice and peeled zest of 1 lemon

500g (1lb 2oz) caster (superfine) sugar

For the filling

1 large leek, chopped

1 onion, chopped

4 smoked pancetta slices, chopped
    (optional but recommended)

10 garlic cloves, chopped

a large pinch of salt, plus extra to season

4 tablespoons flavourless oil, plus 500ml
    (16fl oz) for deep frying

100g (3½oz) salted butter

100g (3½oz) plain (all-purpose) flour

500ml (16fl oz) whole milk

180g (6¼oz) manchego, grated

freshly ground black pepper

For the breadcrumb coating

100g (3½oz) plain (all-purpose) flour

2 eggs, beaten with a dash of whole milk

200g (7oz) panko breadcrumbs

01 First, make the quince jam. Core the quinces and dice the flesh, skin on, into pieces.

02 Place the cores into a large saucepan. Pulse the flesh in a food processor until small, then tip the pieces into the pan with the cores. Cover with just enough water to submerge the fruit.

03 Use a knife to remove any white pith from the strips of lemon zest. Place the peel into the pan with the quince and place over a low heat. Bring to a simmer and cook for 1–1½ hours, until the quince has completely softened.

04 Pour the mixture through a sieve, catching the liquid in a jug. Reserve the pulp and peel. Pour half the liquid into a saucepan and add the sugar (discard the remaining liquid). Tip in the pulp and peel and place over a low heat. Bring to a simmer and cook for 20 minutes, until reduced slightly and the quince begins to look opaque.

05 Remove the lemon peel from the jam, then use a hand-held stick blender to blitz to a paste. I like my quince jam to have a little bit of texture, but you could strain it through a sieve again to make it smoother. Pour the hot jam into a sterilized jar. Leave to cool.

06 Make the croquettes. Pulse the leek, onion, pancetta and garlic in a food processor to a fine paste. (Or, very finely chop the ingredients.) Add the salt and oil and pulse (or stir) again. Tip the mixture into a large saucepan over a medium–low heat, place the lid on top and sweat for 10–15 minutes, until the mixture smells sweet and aromatic. *To make Nana's Chicken and Broccoli Bake (see page 208), transfer half the mixture to an airtight container. Leave to cool.*

07 Add the salted butter to the mixture in the pan and allow to melt. Whisk in the flour and keep whisking for 3–4 minutes to cook out the flour. Whisk in the milk, a little at a time, to a smooth sauce. Add the manchego and keep whisking until the mixture is smooth and the consistency of mashed potato. Season well.

08 Turn off the heat. *To make Nana's Chicken and Broccoli Bake, transfer half the mixture to the container with the cooled leek mixture. Refrigerate for up to 2 days.* Place the remaining cheese mixture into a container and cover it with cling film. Refrigerate for at least 1 hour, to cool.

09 Remove the croquette mixture from the fridge and roll it into about 16 golf-ball-sized balls.

10 Gather three bowls for the coating: fill one with the flour, one with the egg mixture and one with the breadcrumbs. One by one, coat the balls in flour, then egg mixture, then breadcrumbs, repeating the whole sequence – flour, egg, breadcrumbs – to form a double coating before moving on to the next ball. (If you don't want to cook all the croquettes at once, you can store them in an airtight container and freeze them for up to 1 month – they will cook from frozen.)

11 To cook the croquettes, pour the 500ml (16fl oz) of oil into a large, heavy-based saucepan and heat it until it reaches 180°C (350°F) on a cooking thermometer, or until a cube of day-old bread sizzles and turns golden in 1 minute. (Alternatively, use a deep-fat fryer.) Add the croquettes to the hot oil, 4 at a time, and fry for 3–4 minutes, until golden. Remove each batch with a slotted spoon and set aside to drain on kitchen paper while you cook the remainder.

12 To serve, transfer the croquettes to a serving plate or bowl, with a few tablespoons of the quince jam alongside for dipping. *To serve the Perfectly Balanced Cheese Board with Quince Jam (see page 211), refrigerate the remaining jam for up to 1 month.*

Vampire Lamb

Serves 4

3 hours 15 minutes

1.7kg (3lb 12oz) bone-in lamb shoulder
8 garlic cloves
1 small bunch of chives, roughly chopped
75ml (2½fl oz) olive oil
18 black garlic cloves
6 rosemary sprigs, each cut into 3 pieces
salt and freshly ground black pepper

01 Remove the lamb from the fridge 1 hour before you intend to roast it – this allows it to come up to room temperature and cook evenly once it goes into the oven.

02 Preheat the oven to 240°C (220°C fan/475°F/Gas 8).

03 In a food processor (or in a mortar with a pestle), pulse (or grind) the regular garlic cloves, chives and olive oil to make a paste. Season well with salt and pepper.

04 Place the lamb into a baking tray, then, using a sharp knife, make 18 small holes all over it and gently push the black garlic cloves into them. Using a spoon, cover the lamb with half the garlic and chive paste. Skewer the rosemary pieces into the holes with the black garlic.

05 Place the roasting tray into the oven and roast the lamb for 1 hour. Then, remove from the oven and discard the rosemary sprigs. Cover the tray tightly with foil, taking care as it will be hot.

06 Reduce the heat to 200°C (180°C fan/400°F/Gas 6) and return the lamb to the oven for a further 2 hours, until it is tender and falling apart. ***To make the Sesame Lamb Dumplings (see page 212) and the Date and Lamb Tagine (see page 213), transfer 400g (14oz) of the lamb meat to an airtight container. Refrigerate for up to 4 days, or freeze for up to 1 month (defrost before using).*** Rest the remaining lamb for 10–15 minutes before carving and serving.

Mapled Cream
Kale *with* Paneer

Serves 4

35 minutes

2 tablespoons flavourless oil

2 onions, finely chopped

3cm (1¼in) piece of fresh ginger, peeled
     and finely chopped

6 garlic cloves, finely chopped

300g (10oz) kale, tough stems removed,
     leaves sliced into 1cm (½in) strips

1½ teaspoons garam masala

1½ teaspoons ground coriander

4 tablespoons maple syrup or runny honey

150g (5½oz) paneer, cut into 2cm (¾in)
     cubes

200ml (7fl oz) double (heavy) cream

salt and freshly ground black pepper

01 Heat the oil in a large frying pan over a low heat. When hot, add the onions, ginger and garlic and season generously with salt. Fry the mixture for 7–8 minutes, until the garlic smells sweet and the onions have softened. Tip the mixture into a bowl and set it aside.

02 Immediately tip the kale into the frying pan, season with salt and fry it over a high heat, stirring occasionally, for 8–10 minutes. Add a splash of water and cook the greens for a further 4–5 minutes, until tender. Add the onion mixture back into the pan.

03 Once most of the liquid has evaporated from the pan, add the garam masala and coriander and cook for 1–2 minutes to lightly toast the spices. Add the maple syrup or honey and the paneer, then pour in the cream, stirring as you go. Cook for 3–4 minutes to warm through, then season to taste with salt and pepper before serving. ***To make the Peshwari Swirls (see page 214), transfer 200g (7oz) of the mixture to an airtight container. Separate out a further 2–3 tablespoons into another container to make the Garam Masala Greens and Cheddar Toastie (see page 216). Refrigerate for up to 3 days.***

Mint Butter Potatoes *with* Pomegranate

Serves 4

25 minutes

1kg (2¼lb) new potatoes

2 tablespoons salted butter

a large bunch of mint, leaves picked and
    very finely chopped, plus extra to serve

90ml (3fl oz) tablespoons malt vinegar

2 teaspoons Dijon mustard

salt and freshly ground black pepper

3 tablespoons pomegranate seeds, to serve

01 Bring a large saucepan of salted water to a boil over a high heat. Tip in the potatoes, reduce the heat and simmer for 10–15 minutes, until the potatoes are tender.

02 Meanwhile, melt the butter in a large microwave-safe bowl in the microwave on medium power in 5-second bursts. Stir through the mint and vinegar and set aside.

03 Drain the cooked potatoes and tip them into the bowl with the minted butter, turning to coat. ***To make the Spanish Omelette (see page 216), transfer 8 potatoes to an airtight container. Refrigerate for up to 3 days.***

04 Halve or quarter the potatoes left in the bowl, if you wish, then add the mustard, season with salt and pepper and toss until coated. Sprinkle with a little extra chopped mint and the pomegranate seeds to serve.

Miso Caramel
Banoffee Pie

Serves 6

30 minutes, plus cooling and chilling

For the miso caramel

80g (2¾oz) dark brown soft sugar

80g (2¾oz) unsalted butter

½ teaspoon vanilla paste

300ml (10fl oz) double (heavy) cream

1 heaped tablespoon brown miso

For the caramelized banana

1 teaspoon unsalted butter

1 banana, halved lengthways

3 tablespoons dark brown soft sugar

To assemble

1 large, sweet pastry case

600ml (1 pint) double (heavy) cream

3 ripe bananas, cut into 2cm (¾in) slices

2 teaspoons ground cinnamon

1 tablespoon caster (superfine) sugar

01 Make the miso caramel filling. Tip the dark brown soft sugar into a medium saucepan over a high heat. Cook, without stirring, until the edges of the sugar begin to melt, then add the butter. Stir vigorously – don't worry if the sugar hardens. Keep stirring and it will soften again.

02 Once the sugar and butter have melted together fully, add the vanilla and the 300ml (10fl oz) of double (heavy) cream – again, keep stirring, this time until the caramel comes together and is smooth.

03 Stir in the miso and whisk to combine, then leave until the mixture has been bubbling for 1 minute. Remove the pan from the heat and pour the caramel into a heatproof container. Leave to cool. **To make the Banana and Miso Caramel Frappé (see page 217), spoon 1 tablespoon of the cooled caramel into an airtight container. Refrigerate for up to 3 days.**

04 Make the caramelized banana. Melt the butter in a frying pan over a low heat. Place the banana halves, cut side down, in the pan and add the sugar. Leave the sugar to melt, then turn the banana halves gently to coat. Remove them from the pan and set aside to cool.

05 To assemble, line the pastry case with the slices of banana. Add a thick layer of the cooled caramel over the top. Refrigerate for 10 minutes to firm up slightly.

06 Pour the 600ml (1 pint) of double cream into a large mixing bowl. Add the cinnamon and caster (superfine) sugar and use a hand-held electric whisk to whip the cream mixture just until it holds soft peaks.

07 Just before serving, spoon the sweet cinnamon cream on top of the miso caramel and decorate with the caramelized banana halves. Serve in slices. Refrigerate any leftovers in an airtight container for up to 3 days.

NANA'S CHICKEN AND BROCCOLI BAKE

When we were young, my sister and I loved having supper at my grandparents' house, partly because of Nana's chicken and broccoli bake. Nana makes hers slightly differently to this one, though – as she passionately reminded me when I asked her if I could include it in the book. Nana uses a can of condensed chicken soup in place of the sauce and covers her bake in cheese. This recipe is slightly more nuanced (sorry, Nana!), with the leeks and pancetta giving the silky sauce an extra depth. I am, however, still partial to a generous grating of cheese on top, if there's any in the fridge.

Serves 2–4   1 hour

150g (5½oz) leek and manchego sauce from Manchego Croquettes with Quince Jam (see page 200)
1 tablespoon medium curry powder
2 bone-in, skin-on chicken breasts
2 bone-in, skin-on chicken legs
1 lemon, cut into wedges
2 tablespoons flavourless oil
1 head of broccoli, broken into florets
100g (3½oz) Brussels sprouts, halved
(or use any greens, chopped, you have to hand)
salt and freshly ground black pepper

01 Preheat the oven to 200°C (180°C fan/ 400°F/Gas 6).

02 Place the sauce in a large baking dish and add the curry powder. Mix well.

03 Place the chicken pieces and lemon wedges on top and drizzle with the oil, then sprinkle generously with salt and pepper to season. Place in the centre of the oven for 30 minutes, until the chicken is beginning to brown. Remove the dish from the oven, then remove the chicken pieces to a plate.

04 Add the broccoli and sprouts to the sauce and stir well to combine. Place the chicken back on top and return to the oven for a further 20 minutes, until the chicken is beautifully browned and thoroughly cooked through. Serve straight away.

PERFECTLY BALANCED CHEESE BOARD WITH QUINCE JAM

While you might think that a cheese board isn't exactly a recipe, a well-balanced cheese board, perfectly executed, can be the talk of the occasion. I've put together my favourites here for what I think are the best flavour combinations. A wedge of cheddar with a dollop of quince jam is right up there for me; or, a little piece of brie with a wedge of honeydew melon. Goat's cheese and chocolate – trust me – is a conversation starter if you have friends with you.

Serves 4   10 minutes

a wedge of brie
a wedge of your choice of blue cheese
a wedge of cheddar
a wedge of extra-mature gouda
a wedge of soft goat's cheese
runny honey and/or honeycomb
**1 jar of quince jam from Manchego Croquettes
     with Quince Jam (see page 200)**
mixed pickles of your choice
fruit of your choice (I like red seedless grapes, figs
     and honeydew melon)
dark (bittersweet) and/or milk chocolate, broken
     into squares
mixed crackers of your choice

01 Simply arrange all the ingredients on a serving platter or cheese board to allow your guests to self-serve (you can cut the cheeses and fruit into bitesize pieces first, if you like).

SESAME LAMB DUMPLINGS

Dumplings are my go-to comfort food – the comfort comes as much from the making as from the eating. Allow yourself an hour – creating them with care, immersing yourself in the beautiful process. Although I've used lamb in this remix, you can also use leftover cooked chicken, diced beef or even prawns. And, if you make a few too many (if that's even a thing), they freeze very well for up to a month and you can cook them from frozen whenever the craving strikes.

Serves 3–4   1 hour

150g–250g (5½–9oz) Vampire Lamb (see page 203), or any other leftover cooked meat, finely chopped
2 teaspoons ginger paste
1 teaspoon garlic paste
2 carrots, peeled and finely chopped
1 leek, finely chopped
1 teaspoon caster (superfine) sugar
1 teaspoon sesame oil
1 tablespoon light soy sauce
1x 250g packet of dumpling pastry skins
    (about 20 skins)
2 tablespoons flavourless oil

FOR THE DIPPING SAUCE
4 tablespoons light soy sauce
5mm (¼in) piece of fresh ginger, peeled
    and finely chopped
¼ teaspoon sesame oil

01 Place the leftover meat into a large mixing bowl with all the remaining ingredients except for the pastry skins and flavourless oil, and combine well.

02 Take a pastry skin into the palm of your hand and place about 1 teaspoon of the mixture into the middle – don't be tempted to overfill. Dip your finger in a bowl of water and run it around the edge of half the pastry circle. Gently fold the pastry over the filling to form a half-moon shape, and seal together the edges. (There are online tutorials for how to crimp the edges like a pro.) Repeat until you have used up all the filling – you should make about 20 dumplings altogether. (If you don't wish to eat all of the dumplings now, place them, uncooked, in an airtight container. Freeze them for up to 1 month. Cook from frozen.)

03 In a bowl, combine all the ingredients for the dipping sauce and set aside.

04 To cook the dumplings, place the oil into a large, lidded frying pan over a medium heat. When hot, add the dumplings, flat side down, and fry for 2–3 minutes, until the undersides are golden brown. Add 100ml (3½fl oz) of water to the pan, taking care as the water may spit, then place the lid on the pan. Cook for a further 4–5 minutes, then remove the lid and transfer the dumplings to a serving plate. Leave to cool for a moment or two before eating with the dipping sauce alongside.

CHEF'S TIP: If you like, use a food processor to chop the carrots and leek to make them very fine – this will help bring out the flavour in the veg.

DATE AND
LAMB TAGINE

*I've taken inspiration from a traditional
Moroccan tagine for this remix, using the flavour
notes from the sweet dates, fragrant cinnamon
and rich tomatoes. Aside from popping a few
things into a pot, there isn't that much to do – it is
a warming supper, reminiscent of the rooftop
cafés of Marrakesh, with very little effort indeed.
If you don't fancy couscous, serve the tagine with
warmed flat breads instead.*

Serves 2   40 minutes

2 tablespoons flavourless oil
1 onion, grated, or very finely chopped
2 tablespoons garlic paste
4 Medjool dates, pitted and chopped
1 x 400g can of chopped tomatoes
150g (5½oz) Vampire Lamb (see page 203),
    cut into bitesize cubes

FOR THE SPICE MIX
1 teaspoon cayenne pepper
1 teaspoon ground cinnamon
1 teaspoon ground coriander
1 teaspoon sweet smoked paprika
1 teaspoon ground turmeric
1 teaspoon ground white pepper

TO SERVE
150g (5½oz) couscous
200ml (7fl oz) boiling water from a kettle
1 teaspoon freshly ground black pepper
3 tablespoons pomegranate seeds (optional)
a small handful of coriander (cilantro),
    leaves picked (optional)

01 Drizzle the oil into a large saucepan over a low
heat. When hot, add the onion, place a lid on the pan
and sweat for 5 minutes, until the onion begins to
smell sweet and is very lightly browned. Add the
garlic paste and cook, uncovered, for 4 minutes to
bring out the flavour.

02 Meanwhile, combine all the spices for the spice
mix in a bowl. When the mixture in the pan is ready,
add the spice mix and stir quickly to create a paste.
Fry the paste for 2–3 minutes, then add about
3 tablespoons of water to the pan, along with the
chopped dates, tomatoes and lamb. Stir well and
add another 100ml (3½fl oz) of water. Mix, bring to
a simmer, then place the lid on the pan and leave to
simmer over a low heat for 15 minutes, until the
tagine is hot through and the lamb has softened.

03 To serve, tip the couscous into a heatproof bowl
and pour over the boiling water. Mix well, cover,
then leave for 10 minutes for the couscous to
rehydrate and soften. Stir through the black pepper,
and the pomegranate seeds and coriander (cilantro)
leaves (if using). Serve the lamb tagine on a bed of
couscous. (Alternatively, you can dispense with the
couscous and serve the tagine with warmed flat
breads, if you prefer.)

PESHWARI SWIRLS

This remix is quite possibly my favourite of the whole book. Growing up, getting a peshwari naan bread from the local Indian restaurant was the absolute highlight of culinary joy. Soft, warm pillowy bread, wrapped around sweet coconut and almond paste fills me with glee. These Peshwari Swirls encapsulate all of those flavours, and because you've already made the mapled cream kale, they're almost dangerously easy to rustle up. I say dangerous because, once you've made these once, I pretty much guarantee you'll be thinking about when you can make them again (and again).

Makes 7   55 minutes

50g (1¾oz) ground almonds
50g (1¾oz) desiccated (shredded) coconut
200g (7oz) Mapled Cream Kale (see page 204)
1 teaspoon garam masala
1 teaspoon ground coriander
7 sheets of spring roll pastry
1 egg, lightly beaten
1–2 teaspoons nigella seeds (optional)

01 Preheat the oven to 200°C (180°C fan/400°F/ Gas 6).

02 Scatter the almonds and coconut over a baking tray and bake for 4–6 minutes, until golden brown.

03 Place the Mapled Cream Kale in a bowl and add the toasted almonds and coconut along with the garam masala and ground coriander. Mix well, making sure that everything is fully combined.

04 Place 1 pastry sheet on a clean work surface and brush the left edge with beaten egg.

05 Divide the peshwari mixture into 7 equal portions. Spoon 1 portion in a sausage shape along the edge closest to you, leaving about a 2cm (¾in) border. Very carefully fold the pastry edge closest to you over the filling and roll to fully enclose. Then, curve the pastry roll in on itself to form a spiral, tucking the loose end slightly underneath. Repeat with the remaining sheets of pastry and portions of filling to give 7 rolls altogether.

06 Line a baking sheet with greaseproof paper and transfer the swirls on to the paper. Brush with more beaten egg, taking care to get right into the crevices, and finish with a final sprinkling of the nigella seeds (if using). Bake the swirls for 30–35 minutes, until lightly golden. Serve warm or cold.

GARAM MASALA GREENS AND CHEDDAR TOASTIE

Kick back and enjoy a toasted sandwich that wouldn't look out of place at any noteworthy deli. You can omit the mango chutney, if you like, or replace it with any other chutney you have in the fridge. This remix is going to be delicious whatever way and you'll get to say you've eaten your greens.

Serves 1   10 minutes

2 slices of your choice of bread
1 tablespoon mango chutney (optional)
about 20g (¾oz) mature cheddar, grated
**2–3 tablespoons Mapled Cream Kale
    (see page 204)**
2 tablespoons mayonnaise

01 Lay the 2 slices of bread on the work surface. Spread the mango chutney (if using) over 1 slice and sprinkle the cheddar on top. Spread the maple creamed kale on the other slice in an even layer. Bring the topped slices together to sandwich the fillings.

02 Spread 1 tablespoon of mayonnaise over the top of the sandwich.

03 Heat a frying pan over a medium heat until hot. Place the sandwich into the pan, carefully turning it mayo side down. Then, spread the uppermost side with the remaining mayonnaise. After 3–4 minutes, once the underside is toasted, flip the sandwich and cook for a further 3–4 minutes to toast the other side. Remove from the pan and serve straight away.

SPANISH OMELETTE

Making a Spanish omelette is like making a gift for yourself that you can enjoy again and again. Being able to take a wedge from the fridge whenever hunger strikes will make your future self forever grateful. This version is particularly easy, because you've already cooked the potatoes.

Serves 4–6   30 minutes, plus resting

120ml (4fl oz) olive oil
2 shallots or 1 onion, finely sliced
8 eggs
**8 Mint Butter Potatoes (see page 205),
    thinly sliced**
salt and freshly ground black pepper

01 Heat 1 tablespoon of the oil in a large, ovenproof frying pan over a low heat. When hot, add the shallots or onion and cook for 10–15 minutes, until soft and translucent. Set aside.

02 Crack the eggs into a large bowl and gently break them up, but don't whisk them. Add the potatoes, the cooked shallots or onion and 75ml (2½fl oz) of the olive oil and stir to combine. Season with salt and pepper. Preheat the grill (broiler) to medium-high.

03 Heat the remaining oil in the frying pan over a low heat. Pour in the egg mixture, increase the heat to medium–low, stir once, then allow it to settle in the pan. Cook for 6–7 minutes, until firm on the bottom and at the edge, but wobbly in the middle.

04 Transfer the pan to the grill and cook the top of the omelette for 3–4 minutes, until set. I like to leave the omelette for 15 minutes or more before serving to allow it to cool and firm up. Serve in wedges. Slice any leftovers into portions and place them in an airtight container. Refrigerate for up to 2 days.

BANANA AND MISO CARAMEL FRAPPÉ

I'd quite like to put miso caramel in every coffee I make, but sometimes we must practise the art of self-restraint. Still, if making the banoffee pie has given me some spare, it would be rude not to. Coffee and banana are natural best friends and the miso caramel brings that sweet umami richness to really tie everything together. If you're feeling extra fancy, you could swap out half of the ice cubes and add a scoop of vanilla ice cream.

Makes 2   5 minutes

1 teaspoon granulated instant coffee
1 tablespoon boiling water from a kettle
250ml (9fl oz) whole milk
4 ice cubes
1 large banana, sliced into rounds
**1 tablespoon miso caramel from Miso Caramel
    Banoffee Pie (see page 206)**

01 Put the coffee into a large heatproof mug, add the boiling water and stir to dissolve.

02 Pour in the milk and mix well, then tip the mixture into a blender. Add the ice, the banana and the miso caramel and blend until completely smooth. Pour equally into 2 chilled, tall glasses and enjoy!

Index

Acknowledgments

This book wouldn't be possible without the support, encouragement and selfless recipe-tasting of my partner, Iftekar – it is with his encouragement and the words "wow, this is nearly as good as my mum's" that writing these recipes has been such an enjoyable process. I would also like to thank my lifelong business partner and best friend, Ryan Riley, for replying to my 1am messages of "Am I allowed to write this?" and for his creative input. Thanks, too, to my great friend Dayna Brackley, for helping me put together my proposal and her constant enthusiasm; and my lovely friend Steve, ex-front-of-house sparring partner, for giving me his honest opinion in all circumstances.

Thanks to my family, for letting me send endless photo updates of my cooking in the family group chat; and to my therapist, Bob, for listening to and helping me unpick every insecurity I have experienced about writing.

I would also like to thank Stephanie Milner, my commissioning editor, for believing in me and in this book and for giving me the wonderful opportunity to see it come to life. As well as thanks for the constant support from Judy Barratt, the most amazing copy-editor, who helped to make this book into something legible and the process so enjoyable. Thank you to Bess for her guiding hand during the design process and for doing everything she could to make me feel comfortable; to Georgie Hewitt, the book's designer, who has also been my listening ear throughout and has helped me create something gorgeous; and to Anisa Makhoul for the most beautiful illustrations I could have wished for.

Just a couple more before this turns into an Oscar-worthy thank-you list. Thanks to Valerie Berry, my food stylist, who worked incredibly hard to make the images so stunning and was a pleasure to be around; and to Yuki Sugiura, the amazing photographer, who helped the food on the page come to life – your calm and collected way of working was a revelation to me. To Alexander Breeze, the most talented prop stylist I've ever worked with.

Thanks to my cats, Jeremy Sprinkles and Mutton Moot, who accompany me in the kitchen when I'm testing and take over my keyboard while I write.

Thank you to my many sources of inspiration in the food world, who perhaps don't know that I'm constantly enriched by what they create: Nik Sharma, Ixta Belfrage, Mark Weins, Tom Cenci, Milli Taylor, James Dawe, Emmy, John Longland, Thuy Diem Pham, Vanessa Kimbell, Ben Tish, June Xie and Ann Reardon – you are all such wonderful wellsprings of learning for me and I am forever grateful for the content you all create.

And thank you to you, the reader, for buying this book. I hope that the recipes bring you as much joy as they have brought me.

18-06-21.

PILLGWENLLY